Psychology After

Ian Parker has been a leading light in the fields of critical and discursive psychology for over 25 years. The *Psychology After Critique* series brings together for the first time his most important papers. Each volume in the series has been prepared by Ian Parker and presents a newly written introduction and focused overview of a key topic area.

Psychology After Lacan is the sixth volume in the series and addresses three central questions:

- Why is Lacanian psychoanalysis re-emerging in mainstream contemporary psychology?
- What is original in this account of the human subject?
- What implications does Lacanian psychoanalysis have for psychology?

This book introduces Lacan's influential ideas about clinical psychoanalysis and contemporary global culture to a new generation of psychologists. The chapters cover a number of key themes including conceptions of the human subject within psychology, the uses of psychoanalysis in qualitative research, different conceptions of ethics within psychology and the impact of cyberspace on human subjectivity. The book also explores key debates currently occurring in Lacanian psychoanalysis, with discussion of culture, discourse, identification, sexuality and the challenge to mainstream notions of normality and abnormality.

Psychology After Lacan is essential reading for students and researchers in psychology, psychosocial studies, sociology, social anthropology and cultural studies, and for psychoanalysts of different traditions engaged in academic research. It will also introduce key ideas and debates within critical psychology to undergraduates and postgraduate students across the social sciences.

Ian Parker is Professor of Management in the School of Management, University of Leicester, UK, Visiting Professor in the Department of Psychoanalysis, Ghent University, Belgium, and Co-Director of the Discourse Unit, UK (www.discourseunit.com)

Psychology After Critique

Ian Parker has been at the centre of developments in critical and discursive psychology for over 25 years. The *Psychology After Critique* series brings together for the first time his most important and influential papers. Each volume in the series has been prepared by Ian Parker, presents a concise and focused overview of a key topic area, and includes a newly written introduction which traces the continuing impact of the 'crisis', 'deconstruction', 'discourse analysis', 'psychoanalysis' and 'Lacanian research' inside the discipline of psychology.

Volumes in the series:

Psychology After the Crisis
Scientific paradigms and political debate

Psychology After Deconstruction
Erasure and social reconstruction

Psychology After Discourse Analysis
Concepts, methods, critique

Psychology After Psychoanalysis
Psychosocial studies and beyond

Psychology After the Unconscious
From Freud to Lacan

Psychology After Lacan
Connecting the clinic and research

Psychology After Lacan

Connecting the clinic and research

Ian Parker

Routledge
Taylor & Francis Group
LONDON AND NEW YORK

First published 2015
by Routledge
27 Church Road, Hove, East Sussex BN3 2FA

and by Routledge
711 Third Avenue, New York, NY 10017

Routledge is an imprint of the Taylor & Francis Group, an informa business

British Library Cataloguing in Publication Data
A catalogue record for this book is available from the British Library

Library of Congress Cataloging in Publication Data
    Parker, Ian, 1956–
    Psychology after Lacan : connecting the clinic and research /
    Ian Parker.—1 Edition.
    pages cm
    Includes bibliographical references and index.
    1. Psychoanalysis. 2. Psychology.
    3. Lacan, Jacques, 1901–1981. I. Title.
    BF173.P28535 2014
    150.19'5—dc23
    2014009266

ISBN: 978-1-84872-216-3 (hbk)
ISBN: 978-1-84872-217-0 (pbk)
ISBN: 978-1-31577-403-9 (ebk)

Typeset in Times New Roman
by Swales & Willis Ltd, Exeter, Devon

Printed and bound in the United States of America by Publishers Graphics,
LLC on sustainably sourced paper.

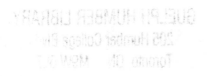

Contents

Series foreword

In the essays collected in these six volumes Ian Parker has brought together for the first time the two radical movements that began in social psychology in the 1960s and 1970s. One of these movements was based on a critical appraisal of the defective methodology of the research programmes that emanated from mainstream American social psychologists. This was rejected for a variety of reasons by a wide variety of critics who shared the belief that people actually deal with what they take to be the meanings of what is happening around them and the significance of the arenas in which actions were performed, according to the rules and conventions of their local social order. The results of a shallow, positivistic approach to discerning the wellsprings of human social behaviour were rejected as sources of reliable knowledge. How people thought, acted, felt and perceived their worlds had little to do with how people actually lived their lives together. People in the stripped-down meaningless worlds of the social psychological experiment were not reacting to stimuli, just trying to make sense of anomic situations with whatever resources their education and history had provided them. People are not empty sites for causal processes but active agents engaged in the tasks and projects that their lives throw up.

At the same time, and for the most part independently, a different kind of criticism was emerging – a display of the moral aspects of the very kind of psychology that was rejected as unscientific by the methodological sceptics. If people believed that psychologists were unearthing the truth about how people thought and acted, then insofar as actual people were unlike this paradigm they would or should strive to achieve it. The realization that such psychology-driven workbooks of human vagaries such as the DSM series of manuals, by presenting a range of ways for human beings to live and act as disorders, defined a kind of person to be emulated who was very much like the bland artefact generated by the statistical methods of the American mainstream, all dissent and difference being ironed out in the deference to some arbitrary level of statistical significance. Critical psychology began to reveal the ways in which the power structures of society and the relations between people from different social classes were brought about. Critical psychology drew from social constructionism the principle that when you can see how something is manufactured you can change it.

The strangest of all the eccentricities of the 'main stream' was the neglect of language. It could hardly be more obvious that the main medium of social interactions is linguistic. Once that is acknowledged the way is open for another dimension – the study of the differences between the linguistically differentiated cultures of the various tribes of humankind. This was not 'cross-cultural psychology' which was merely the transfer of Western middle-class conceptions of life to shape research into the lives of people of very different ways of thinking and acting.

In this elegant introduction to the field of critical psychology Ian Parker shows how gradually but inexorably the two streams began to merge, a process that is continuing. The most striking way in which a critical psychology is currently evolving is in the development of psychology as a moral science. Tied to this insight are explicit studies of the way rights and duties come between natural and acquired tendencies to act and the possibilities that different local moral orders allow: the rapidly growing field of positioning theory.

But all was not plain sailing. The turn to deconstruction, via a reshaping of the linguistic turn to encompass the richer domain of discourse, led to the neglect of the key claim that the 'new psychology' gave socially relative and epoch-specific reliable knowledge, at least pro tem. To reclaim psychiatry from the neurochemists, the place of the active person within a local framework was an essential core to be defended. If persons fade away into clusters of locally contingent selves the key point of the reality of human agency was in danger of being lost.

The second deep insight – perhaps more important than the defence of persons, was relocation of 'mind' to the social network of meaningful interactions, the mind in society. When we learn to abstract ourselves one by one from the social nexus from which each of us emerges we bear with us the indelible mark of our cultural origins. The recoverable content of psycho-dynamics relocates the unconscious to 'what lies between'. In the end we turn back to language and relate symbolic systems not as abstract calculi obeying inbuilt species-specific rules but as the common instruments with which we manage our lives. Psychology can be nothing but the study of cultural-historical-instrumental practices of our ever-changing tribal societies.

The *Psychology After Critique* series is the comprehensive resource we have been waiting for to enable new generations not only of budding psychologists but all those who concern themselves with how we might live, to find their way through the mistakes of the positivistic illusion of a science to a just appreciation of what it might be to come to understand the myriad ways a human being can be a person among persons.

Rom Harré
Linacre College, University of Oxford, UK
Psychology Department, Georgetown University, USA

Series preface

What is psychology? Once upon a time psychologists imagined that they knew the answer to this question. Their object of study, they argued, should be the way that individuals perceive the world, think about it and act in it together with other people. Perception and thinking, in developmental and cognitive psychology, for example, was studied as if it only happened inside the heads of the experimental 'subjects' in scientific laboratories and then 'social psychology' often amounted to little more than an accumulation of the behaviour of those same atomized individuals. The idea that people talked to each other, and that this talk might actually have an effect on the way that people behaved and understood themselves was outside the frame of that kind of academic work.

This series of books is about the consequences of talk being taken seriously, the consequences for scientific investigation and for the way that many researchers today are building innovative new research projects. The discipline of psychology has been transformed since a 'paradigm crisis' erupted nearly half a century ago when pioneers in research into the role of language in thinking and behaviour picked up the thread of early 'radical psychology' critiques which homed in on the limitations of their discipline. The 'paradigm crisis' threw into question the silent world presupposed by the psychologists and launched us all into a world of intense debate over the role of language, of discourse and then of what is shut out of discourse, of the unconscious and of psychoanalysis.

These books were produced in the context of fierce arguments about methods in psychology and over the kinds of concepts we needed to develop in order to do better more radical research. The Discourse Unit was founded in Manchester as a Centre for Qualitative and Theoretical Research on the Reproduction and Transformation of Language, Subjectivity and Practice in 1990. Today it operates as an international trans-institutional collaborative centre which supports a variety of qualitative and theoretical research projects contributing to the development of radical theory and practice. The term 'discourse' is used primarily in critical hermeneutic and structuralist senses to include inquiries influenced by feminism and psychoanalysis. The centre functions as a resource base for qualitative and feminist work, as a support unit for the (re)production of radical academic theory, and as a networking centre for the development of critical perspectives in action research.

We took as our starting point the 'crisis' and the need for critical reflection on the discipline of psychology, the place of psychology and appeals to psychology in other academic disciplines. We then saw the need for a 'critical psychology' that was concerned not only with what went on inside the academic world but also with the way that psychological ideas functioned in the real world outside the universities. The books in this series are written mostly by one individual participant in those debates, but they bring together a number of different arguments for perspectives on the nature of scientific paradigms, deconstruction from literary theory, discourse analysis, psychosocial studies, psychoanalysis and clinical work that were elaborated by researchers in the Discourse Unit.

The books together trace a narrative from the early recognition that language is crucial to understand what is happening in traditional laboratory-experimental psychology – why that kind of psychology is quite useless in telling us about human action – to the development of discourse analysis and the connections with some more radical attempts to 'deconstruct' language from other neighbouring disciplines. A concern with different kinds of psychoanalytic theory – the innovative work now taking place in psychosocial studies – is then introduced to conceptualize the nature of subjectivity. But from the beginning there are some 'red threads' that lead us from the study of language and subjectivity to the study of power and ideology.

These books about psychology as an academic discipline and the increasing role of psychology in our everyday lives are also about the politics of research. And so, when we began to discuss the role of 'deconstruction' or 'psychoanalysis' in the Discourse Unit we always asked whether those other conceptual frameworks would help or hinder us in understanding the connections between knowledge and social change. The books do not pretend to be neutral disinterested description of trends of research in psychology. Our 'crisis' was always about the possibility that the turn to language would also be a turn to more politically engaged – Marxist and feminist – radical reflection on what the theories and methods conceal and what we could open up. The books are accounts of the emergence of key debates after 'the crisis' and sites of 'critical psychological' reflection on the nature of psychology itself.

Ian Parker
Professor of Management in the School of Management,
University of Leicester, and Co-Director of the Discourse Unit
(www.discourseunit.com)

Acknowledgements

This book brings together versions of papers that have either been published in scattered places and are often inaccessible or that are unpublished. Chapter 1 was drawn from my 2003 paper 'Jacques Lacan: Barred Psychologist', *Theory & Psychology*, 13(1), 95–115, doi: 10.1177/0959354303013001764, reprinted by permission of Sage Publications Ltd; Chapter 2 was drawn from my 2001 paper 'Lacan, Psychology and the Discourse of the University', *Psychoanalytic Studies*, 3(1), 67–77, reproduced with permission; Chapter 3 is drawn from my 1995 chapter 'Everyday Behavior(ism) and Therapeutic Discourse: Deconstructing the Ego as Verbal Nucleus in Skinner and Lacan', in J. Siegfried (ed.) *Therapeutic and Everyday Discourse as Behavior Change: Towards a Micro Analysis in Psychotherapy Process Research* (447–467), New York: Ablex, reproduced with permission; Chapter 4 is adapted from my 2009 paper (with Christian Ingo Lenz Dunker as first author) 'How to be Secretly Lacanian in Anti-Psychoanalytic Qualitative Research', *Annual Review of Critical Psychology*, 7, 52–71; Chapter 5 is from Ian Parker, 'Lacanian Ethics in Psychology: Seven Paradigms'. This material was originally published in *Contemporary Theorizing in Psychology: Global Perspectives*, edited by Aydan Gulerce, Arnd Hofmeister, Irmingard Staeuble, Guy Saunders and John Kaye (Concord, ON: Captus University Publications, 2005, www.captus.com), reprinted with permission; and Chapter 6 is drawn from my 2007 paper 'Psychoanalytic Cyberspace, Beyond Psychology', *The Psychoanalytic Review*, 94(1), 63–82, copyright Guilford Press, reprinted with permission of The Guilford Press. I have modified some formulations in the published papers and excluded extraneous material. I am, as ever, grateful to Erica Burman and my colleagues in the international network around the Discourse Unit for their critical comments and support during the preparation of this volume. The mistakes must surely in some way be theirs too.

Introduction

Psychology after Lacan

This book, Volume 6 of the series *Psychology After Critique*, is about the impact of Lacan on the way we think about theory and methodology in psychology. It provides an introduction to Lacan's ideas in relation to clinical psychoanalysis and in relation to contemporary culture. Though the clinical origins and reference points in Jacques Lacan's work are crucial – and I emphasize these through the course of the book – I believe that Lacanian psychoanalysis gives us a particular opportunity to reflect on the historical origins of the clinic as a specific kind of apparatus in which one person – the 'analysand' (as the client or patient is called) – speaks to another, the psychoanalyst (Dunker, 2010; Parker, 2011b).

Lacanian psychoanalysis, as with any other kind of clinical work, constitutes the objects and subjects of its practice to make the approach function, and so we need to approach the theory with something very like the 'social constructionist' spirit that animates much research in critical psychology today (Burr, 2003). This book, like the others in the series, is oriented towards the emerging field of 'critical psychology' (Parker, 2011a). It should be read alongside the other books, which focus in more detail on the paradigm crisis in the discipline in the late 1960s and early 1970s, on the use of deconstruction and discourse analysis as critical resources in qualitative research, and on the impact of psychoanalytic ideas which have prompted the development of 'psychosocial studies'.

In this introduction I briefly review the place of the work of Lacan (2006) in the world of psychoanalysis, and then go on to show how Lacanians develop Freud's (1953–1974) work on the unconscious and sexuality and continue the early psychoanalytic concern with social and personal questioning of self and society. The particular focus on language in Lacan's psychoanalysis is addressed, and his conception of symptoms, diagnosis and the questions that someone asks of their distress when they come to psychoanalysis are outlined. The arguments that Lacan elaborated concerning the direction of the treatment, transference and interpretation and the position of the analyst are discussed, and I then show how the importance that Lacanians give to the notion of 'difference' at the end of the treatment has consequences for the way that we practise psychoanalysis.

Through this account, and in the chapters in the main body of the book, you will be able to see why Lacanian psychoanalysis is now appearing in psychology, and the way the radically different image of the individual it presents not only challenges fundamental assumptions about research in the discipline itself but also the increasing 'psychologization' of contemporary culture (De Vos, 2012). This introduction begins the task, which is taken forward in more detail in the first chapter of the book, of showing the alternative innovative account Lacanian psychoanalysis gives of the human subject, and we are then in a position to appreciate implications for psychology as a separate discipline. So, who was Lacan, what did he have to say, and why is he so important?

Lacan and the turn to language in psychoanalysis

Lacan trained first as a psychiatrist, and he practised as a doctor and psychiatrist later in life (working at one point as the personal physician to the painter Picasso). He trained as a psychoanalyst in Paris in the 1930s, and became a leader of the French section of the International Psychoanalytical Association (IPA). Profound disagreements about theoretical issues (what he saw as the attempt to adapt people to society in US 'ego-psychology') and over questions of practice (IPA objections to deviations in the length of psychoanalytic sessions) led to a decision by the IPA in 1963 that he should not be permitted to train analysts. In 1964 he founded his own school, and following his death in 1981, Lacanian psychoanalysis has spread throughout the world (Roudinesco, 1990).

There are still fierce battles over the role of Lacan's work within psychoanalysis, though in most countries now (particularly in Latin America) supporters of Lacan are in the majority, and Lacanian ideas are an accepted part of psychoanalytic debate. I know of senior IPA analysts in Latin America now going outside their own organization for a second analysis with Lacanians, and there has been friendly contact between the different traditions. An important example of the IPA opening itself, in Argentina, to different traditions is the 1996 encounter between Horacio Etchegoyen, then IPA president, and Jacques-Alain Miller of the Association Mondiale de Psychanalyse (Miller and Etchegoyen, 1996). In Britain there have been fruitful dialogues between Lacanians and followers of Melanie Klein (Burgoyne and Sullivan, 1997).

Lacanians are first of all Freudians, and the kinds of questions we ask in analysis and supervision are rooted in the theoretical frameworks we find in Freud's writing (Benvenuto and Kennedy, 1986). I say 'frameworks' in the plural because although there have been many attempts to tie down what Freud really said, Freud said a good number of different things. Psychoanalysis changed while Freud was alive, and it is still changing. But to work psychoanalytically we must take seriously two things.

First, the *unconscious*. Psychoanalytic treatment rests on the assumption that there is more to human existence than what we are immediately aware of or what we can easily retrieve from our memory. Something in our lives escapes our conscious control, and that means that one of the tasks of analysis is to bring to awareness at least the sense that when we speak we say more than we mean. Slips of the tongue, dreams and jokes are the signs of something other to us, something other which determines how we respond to things and who we think we are. So, in analysis we are looking for signs of the work of the unconscious in the speech of the 'analysand'. The 'analysand' is our term for the 'patient' or 'client' because they are analysing, analysing themselves.

The second thing we must take seriously is *sexuality*. Not so much sexuality as it appears in adult life, as something that seems to have a fixed point of origin and stable object, though that idea about sexuality is quite important, but sexuality as something that drives us into sensuous desirous relations with other people and something that presents us with puzzles about what sexual difference is and what do with it. So, in analysis we are looking at the organization of desire and how our analysand is trying to deal with those relations and solve those puzzles.

Psychoanalysis is subversive. This is where Lacan starts to become really important, because what his reading of psychoanalysis does is to bring to the fore that radical unravelling of human experience that Freud opened up (Nobus, 1998). This is also where he starts to appeal to critical research in psychology. Psychoanalysis is not *only* subversive, of course. Psychoanalytic theory has often been used to pathologize people who do not fit in, or those who refuse to accept dominant definitions of how their desire should be organized. Lacanian psychoanalysis has itself been marginalized in the English-speaking clinical world partly because it refuses the model of the individual, and of the ego as the captain of the soul, that the mainstream analytic tradition here demands. But what we are starting to see now is the re-emergence of Lacan's work, and growing awareness that around half of practising psychoanalysts in the world, if we include those working in France, Spain and Latin America, are Lacanian.

There is clearly a political aspect to this subversive role of psychoanalysis. There is a connection with radical politics, a connection that the early psychoanalytic movement in Freud's day had made. There is a connection with a radical political understanding of the way contemporary institutions try to tame psychoanalysis. And there is a connection with what we could see as a radical personal politics of self-understanding and transformation that the analysand embarks upon. Lacanian psychoanalysis is the practice of that self-understanding and transformation, and that is why it avoids quick fixes, suggestion or the attempt to bring about identification between analysand and analyst.

And this is why, although Lacanian psychoanalysis includes therapeutic moments, it goes far beyond the usual psychotherapeutic aims of developing coping strategies, or recasting problems into more positive thinking. You could say that it is the space for 'deconstructing' how someone copes and how their problems are bound up with the way they think.

Lacan's work is best known for its concern with language as the phenomenon that marks off human beings as speaking beings from other animals (Fink, 1995). It is the acquisition of language, and so the acquisition of a position within the symbolic domain of human culture, that is the necessary condition for communication with others, and at the same time language is the medium that frustrates and sabotages the possibility of direct contact with others and with our objects of desire. As we speak we are also brought into relation with what we cannot say, realms of discourse that are 'other', that are unconscious to us. This is one meaning of Lacan's (1964/1973: 131) dictum 'the unconscious is the discourse of the Other'.

It is the speech of the analysand that reveals to us, and to them, how they have become a conscious being in the world through a certain articulation of language. It is how they have been articulated in the symbolic order that determines how they speak for themselves and how they speak to others, including us. That articulation of elements of the symbolic, their defining 'signifiers' – the elements of language – also defines for them what objects of desire their lives and symptoms revolve around, including a key desired lost object.

This means that the analysis does not search below the surface of language for the meaning of things, though fantasies about what lies below the surface will be very important, but we keep our attention on what is said, on the chains of signifiers. This also means that the questions that will be asked about what has gone on in a session always attend to what was actually said, rather than 'feelings' that may be conjured into place below or behind the symbolic which seem to explain what is happening.

The problematic paradoxical relation to language is exactly what may bring someone to an analyst one day. The particular way in which we entered language structures the way we will experience distress (Nobus, 2000). And psychoanalysis as a 'talking cure' also takes place as a problematic paradoxical relation to an Other, the analyst, within language. This means that the formulation of what the 'problem' might be is, from the beginning, framed by a particular kind of relation to an Other. What we call an analytic 'symptom', then, is something that appears under transference.

We want to know not only what the focus of the analysis might be but also why the problem has emerged now as a 'symptom' that is failing to function. This symptom is not viewed as if it were an expression of an organic disease, to be treated as such or to be traced to an underlying condition that can be cleared up so that the symptom will disappear. The question at the early points in the analysis, then, is not so much what work the symptom does and how it causes so much suffering to the subject, this human subject, as why it is *failing* to work.

We all love our symptoms so much that something must be going wrong for us to be brought to the point where we might be tempted to take them in for repair, and we may want them repaired so they can carry on performing their function for us. The presentation of the symptom to an analyst opens up the possibility for analysis, then, but the demand for analysis then has to be powerful enough to take the analysand to the point where they are willing to ask what this symptom means to them and to be willing to risk giving it up.

The first stages of an analysis and supervision revolve around the question of clinical structure. One of the most important decisions a Lacanian psychoanalyst must make is whether this person who turns up for help is in a state to unravel who they are, or whether it is wiser to assist them in weaving more closely together their sense of self (Fink, 1997).

Lacanians make a categorical distinction for analytic purposes between neurotic structure, which is characterized by repression as the main mode of defence, perverse structure characterized by disavowal, and psychotic structure that is initiated by the most extreme early defence of 'foreclosure'. Because that extreme early defence of foreclosure is a dramatic refusal to be of the symbolic order, certain fundamental signifiers that operate to mediate between self and others are not present. Then a delusory system may be developed, quite successfully perhaps, to function in the place of those fundamental signifiers. We attend to those parts in the speech of the analysand where things seem a little too sure set, a little too certain, and to those parts of speech that seem marked by imaginary phenomena of narcissistic mirroring and rivalry. When the system they have constructed fails to function, the analytic work with someone with psychotic structure is to help them elaborate and develop that system. To undermine or unravel the way they hold their reality in place would be disastrous.

The decision about psychotic structure is not made quickly or completely. And Lacanians will spend the first months, maybe many months, talking face to face with an analysand. We do not invite someone to move onto the couch, to move into that rather disturbing position of speaking to someone whom you cannot see, without being fairly sure that this disturbance will be productive.

Although Lacanians expect to find neurotic, perverse and psychotic traits in everyone, there is not the same notion of a continuum of psychotic experience that there is in some other traditions of psychoanalysis. But neither is there a notion of 'normal' structure, for the entry into the symbolic is always problematic, and it always calls for some measure of defence. Such questions are intimately connected with questions of gender (Verhaeghe, 1999).

These modes of defence are crucial for Lacanians precisely because it is the entry into the symbolic order that constitutes the unconscious as a kind of underside of language, as the system of gaps in our speech. And when we are articulated by language in that kind of way, as subjects with neurotic structure, our existence is also organized by questions about what our place in language is. The diagnosis, then, homes in on those questions and the way they are articulated in analysis so that we can make finer-grain distinctions that will help us gauge how the analysis may progress.

Lacan picks up the Freudian distinction between obsessional neurosis and hysteria. Obsessional neurosis, which is more stereotypically masculine, revolves around questions of existence and death, and guilt. The questions 'Why am I here, and by what right?' can be worried away at, with possible answers and doubts set up that can sometimes make the analysis difficult because they are so closed in together on themselves, like a labyrinth.

Hysteria, which is more stereotypically feminine, is organized around the question of sex and gender, and accusation. 'What is a woman, and what does a woman want?' for example, are questions about the nature of desire, sexual identity and what the Other wants, and these are questions that bring us closer to the kinds of questions the analysand asks of the self and other in analysis.

Direction of the treatment

We do not guide the analysand, but we do guide the direction of the treatment, and this is not done by giving them education or telling them how their lives make sense (Nobus and Quinn, 2005). This is why we need a theoretical framework to make sense of how someone might take to the analytic work, or not. In the case of psychotic structure, the direction of the treatment will be towards the elaboration of a sense of self and reality, a work of construction rather than deconstruction. In the case of perverse structure we do not expect to find a question posed by the subject because they have installed a fetish of some kind through which they organize their enjoyment. And for that reason we do not expect someone of this kind who knows what they want and knows what the Other wants to demand analysis.

In our analytic work with those showing neurotic suffering around the symptoms it is important not to close down what has started to open up. To guide the direction of the treatment is not to impose agendas or to suggest how the work should be done, but to encourage a questioning and self-questioning. The interventions of the analyst point to something beyond what is said, to the fact that there is an unconscious, that the analysand does not have complete control over their words.

The analysand will be invited to follow the Freudian rule of free association in order to bring to light the role of the unconscious. An obsessional strategy to avoid this rule would be to bring the analyst into the labyrinth of choices and doubts that holds things in place. So the analyst will be contributing the kinds of questions and ambiguous comments that throw this strategy off track. These interventions are designed to bring about a 'hystericization' of the subject, so that the direction of the treatment is then all the more the direction of the analysand towards their truth.

The analysand is speaking to us under transference (Nasio, 1998). That is, with assumptions and expectations that are based on past relationships, and these assumptions and expectations frame what they say. They have little else to go on, for they do not know who we really are, and so the transference relationship reveals something of their relation to others. In psychoanalysis transference is a love relationship, and for Lacanians that relationship is to knowledge, as a love of knowledge. The signs of transference, then, are those points when the analysand speaks to the Other, the analyst, as someone who knows something; the analysand supposes a subject who knows.

It is important that the analyst keeps that space open and indeterminate, because we are concerned with what the analysand *supposes*. This is why interpretations should not seem to offer knowledge and so to close down the relationship such that it is defined by what the analyst knows. Lacanians do not, as a rule, make interpretations of the transference. The analyst does actually make comments and allusions about the transference relationship, but these are usually ambiguous in order to open up possibilities for different positions to emerge. The ending of a session at a point that has not been determined in advance is one way of making an interpretation that marks something in a way that is ambiguous. The analysand is the one who is speaking most of the time, the one who is analysing, and so the role of interpretation is to open the possibilities for the analysand to interpret.

We need a theoretical framework not only to guide the direction of the treatment but also to know what place we have in it (Feldstein *et al.*, 1996). Supervision is a place to elaborate that theoretical framework and to track as much what the analyst is in the speech of the analysand as what the analyst wants to say next.

For Lacan (1964/1973: 38), 'desire is desire of the Other'. But there are forms of mutual recognition in the analytic encounter that can lead to things getting stuck or to a positive relationship flipping into a negative one. We need to shift the focus of recognition from imaginary mirror-like relations of identification or rivalry – which are the kinds of relations that face-to-face communication encourages – into the broader questions of recognition of the Other in the symbolic realm. So we are often asking ourselves whether the chains of signifiers in analysis are running along the line of the imaginary or whether we are opening them into the symbolic.

Entry into the symbolic brings about the sense that there is some access to power, perhaps power that has been lost, and that this is a power that is located in the symbolic. There is also then a sense that an object of desire has been lost, an object that may be located somewhere in an Other. This object is what we see in an Other when we fall in love.

So the analyst needs to be aware of the temptation to 'understand' exactly what the analysand is saying, which would mean getting drawn into the line of the imaginary. They need to notice how they are positioned by the analysand in the symbolic, to notice who the analysand is speaking to and where they are speaking from. And the analyst needs to know how they will at points stand in the position of that lost object for the analysand.

What is the end of analysis? To answer this question with a neat formulation would close up the specific answers that each analysand may articulate. We need to ensure that it is the truth of the analysand that emerges and not merely our knowledge. But some theoretical understanding of language and love is necessary for analysis to work (Feldstein *et al.*, 1995).

The entry into the symbolic is Lacan's Oedipal myth, and it brings with it a relation to power, an impossible paradoxical relation to power that Lacan characterizes, in a transformation of Freudian theory, as a relation to the 'phallus'. As we enter language to get into relation with others we lose that relation to others. And as we enter the symbolic to get access to the phallus we are powerless; there is a symbolic castration. The powerlessness, the child's lack in the face of language and the fantasy that language will be access to power, is a matter that is, of course, suffused with questions of gender. These specific issues of sexual difference may be the key issues for an analysand.

In analysis we are confronted with the nature of language as the system of differences that makes us who we are. We also learn something about what language is. Instead of trying to find the one substantial thing that will give us power, a phallus, or tracking down that object of desire that we sense we lost, we discover how our particular fantasy of power and the nature of our object were constructed for us and by us in language. Lacan at one point formulates the work of analysis as to obtain 'absolute difference'. As if only at that point that we are able to give up what has held us in thrall will we be able to do something different with our lives, and then we will perhaps be different too.

Lacanian clinical work has similarities to other forms of psychoanalysis, but the theoretical framework leads the analyst to attend to certain kinds of issues in the course of the treatment. Interlocking concepts enable the analyst to engage with different kinds of clinical practice (Evans, 1996).

The first meetings focus on history and symptoms. Like other psychodynamic approaches, there is dialogue about the nature of the problem and a sense of what the person hopes to get out of the encounter. One important question, given that symptoms give some enjoyment, is 'why now?' – what is it that has become too much to bear and what opens possibilities of change? There is also attention to the possibility that the person would be thrown into crisis by analysis – may suffer a 'psychotic break' – and if that were the case the therapeutic work in the preliminary interviews would continue and the emphasis would be on the construction or reinforcement of a symbolic system rather than its questioning and unravelling.

Like other psychodynamic approaches, the task of the patient is to free associate, to say anything that comes to mind, however stupid or unpleasant. The overall course of analysis is not fixed in advance with a determinate number of sessions, and analysis may be thought of as ending when the person stops turning up. The length of each session is not fixed, but the end of a session, with a certain average length, will be at a point where something important is said or left unsaid. The end of the session is a kind of interpretation.

The distinctive Lacanian theoretical framework enables the therapist to make sense of what is going on, rather than leading to dramatically different interventions. Interpretation is designed to keep free association going and to open the unconscious to further elaboration. This means that comments that link ideas may be ambiguous rather than trying to fix things. This also means that transference (and counter-transference as part of transference) is not interpreted directly; there is no interpretation *of* the transference because this would close things down, but the notion is used by the therapist as a frame and so there is interpretation *in* the transference.

Analysis should enable the person to loosen their strong attachment to the symptom, and to find another position in relation to their symbolic world. The ethos, then, is one of questioning how we have come to be the way we are, understanding something of the key points in which we have become the person we are, what our desire is, for what, and whose it is. Through this process analysis explores what relation we adopt to others.

Conclusions, about therapy and theory, and psychology

In some ways Lacanian psychoanalysis is incompatible with psychotherapy, and with psychiatry and psychology for that matter (Parker, 2011b). The encounter between analyst and analysand (who is usually positioned in therapeutic discourse as the 'patient' or 'client') will of course include elements of therapy and even of counselling. But the unravelling of the self and of a narrative of personal history that holds a sense of identity in place may be unbearable. This task of reflexive deconstruction that an analysand embarks upon in psychoanalysis is very difficult, and they may hesitate at times for good reason, or for bad reasons that it may be necessary to honour. There are a number of points of difference between psychoanalysis and psychotherapy, and with the image that psychologists have of the therapeutic process in counselling that we should note here.

An attempt to attain *empathy* could serve to sabotage what is most radical about psychoanalysis, for the sense that one has empathized with another serves to make them the same as oneself. If we try to bring about some form of *harmonization* between aspects of the self this could serve to cover over the contradictions that make someone into a human subject in the first place. The notion that we should try to avoid illusions and instead bring about a more *veridical* relation to the external reality may serve only to obscure the ways in which every image of 'reality' is always already suffused with fantasy. The claim that we should search under the surface of spoken interaction and *excavate* a deeper reality behind language serves to mislead us as to where the unconscious is and how it works. The idea that we should *educate* someone about what is right or wrong or as to how they should understand is one that is particularly problematic for Lacanian psychoanalysis, for it can all too easily turn therapy into the privilege of an expert. If we attempt to *normalize* certain kinds of behaviour or experience it may in the short term bring relief, but this could operate to adapt the subject all the more efficiently to an idea of what is normal. The intention to treat certain kinds of behaviour or experience as *pathological* often transforms them from things that the analyst may not understand into elements of a moral and moralizing narrative. To render treatment into a process that can be made susceptible to *prediction* as part of 'evidence-based' practice serves to close off what is most illuminating about the work of analysis. Finally, if we aim to promote *rationality* as the touchstone of conscious understanding this may serve to divide rationality from irrationality, and to reify both.

The best work in the Lacanian tradition learns from theory and practice in a dialogue with other traditions from psychoanalysis as it has developed in different parts of the world (Shingu, 2004). The secondary literature on Lacan's work in relation to clinical practice is now substantial. Clinicians interested in exploring these ideas are in a position to go back to Lacan's own texts, which have hitherto been quite difficult for those not well versed in the theory, and which have often been badly translated. New translations of key texts into English now make it easier for readers who have trained in the Anglo-American tradition to compare the secondary accounts with Lacan's writings (Lacan, 2006).

You can see that Lacan poses a radical challenge to psychology, and you will see in the following chapters how the clinical work connects with critical psychological research in a number of surprising and fruitful ways. You should also now be able to see that, although his is a strange approach to the human subject, it is not as unbearably difficult to understand as it is sometimes made out to be (Leader and Groves, 1995). This takes us in new directions in the discipline, and allows us to do something very different.

1   Jacques Lacan

Barred psychologist

This first chapter reviews a series of contradictions between the discipline of psychology and what Lacan had to say about the human subject. It thus takes us beyond an 'introduction' to Lacan for psychologists to provide an introduction to alternative critical psychological, even 'anti-psychological' ways of thinking about who we are. Lacan is characterized here with reference to the elaboration of his theoretical and clinical work, with the focus primarily on his own writings. I go quite systematically through the way that Lacan's account of ostensibly 'psychological' questions, such as personality and memory, is quite different from the way that psychologists usually understand them.

What I mean by 'psychology' here is the academic and professional domain of theory and practice developed in Western, specifically Anglo-American culture to describe and explain behavioural and mental processes. It is worth bearing in mind that some other psychological traditions outside the English-speaking world, particularly in Latin America, have drawn on Lacan's work. I also show how Lacan's work differs from apparently 'critical' approaches, like discursive psychology, inside the discipline.

There is such fundamental incompatibility between Lacan's work and psychological views of the individual subject that attempts to assimilate the two traditions are misconceived. This means that psychologists looking to Lacan for answers must question underlying assumptions about theory and methodology in their discipline if they are to take his work seriously. The incompatibility between Lacan and psychology also has important consequences for clinical psychologists who may wish to adopt ideas from the Lacanian tradition, for it highlights the dangers that psychology holds for psychoanalysis if psychological theories and methodologies are taken on good coin. The motif of Lacan as 'barred psychologist' is designed to emphasize these arguments as well as the distinctive account of the human subject that his work entails.

There have been a number of recent attempts to repair the lost historical links between psychology and psychoanalysis, and the work of Lacan is increasingly invoked as an alternative analytic tradition that might appeal to psychologists. In some cases there is a reaching across from psychology into Lacan's work as a resource (e.g. Frosh, 1997), and there are also some attempts to bridge the gap by those more directly involved in Lacanian practice (e.g. Malone and Friedlander, 2000). However, the way the appeal to Lacan functions in this renewed communication between psychoanalysis and psychology is largely through *miscommunication*. It risks indulging an imaginary misrecognition of what Lacan actually has to say to psychologists concerning the assumptions they make about the human subject and what they do.

As we know, Lacan trained first as a psychiatrist (and practised as such through the rest of his life), and then as a psychoanalyst in Paris in the 1930s. Disagreements about theoretical issues (particularly the development of US 'ego-psychology') and questions of practice (particularly over short and variable-length analytic sessions) led to his eventual exclusion from the International Psychoanalytic Association (IPA), an 'excommunication' effected by the demand that he should not train analysts. Since his death in 1981, the Lacanian orientation has grown to now inform the practice of about half the psychoanalysts in the world, with the main concentration being in the Latin countries. This skewed geographical distribution of psychoanalysis facilitates the attempts of the US-based IPA often still to deny Lacan's contribution.

This chapter addresses the problem from a certain position, with a certain address in mind. The question of from where I speak and to whom I am speaking is particularly important in this context, for psychology operates on a model of science that often excludes an attention to the subjectivity of those involved in it as researchers, while for Lacan (1986/1992: 19), 'psychology . . . is nothing more than a mask, and sometimes even an alibi, of the effort to focus on the problem of our own action'. My training is as an academic psychologist working with 'critical' perspectives in the discipline and with psychoanalysis outside it. This chapter is primarily directed to psychologists who may be curious about Lacan but who know little about his work, and this means that the argument does risk already adopting a language that reconfigures subjectivity as something 'psychological'. The effort to render Lacanian concepts intelligible to an audience of psychologists may thus perform the very problem that the chapter revolves around: that Lacan may be thought to be compatible with psychology.

The purpose of this chapter is to review how Lacan approaches domains of human experience traditionally studied by psychology. The argument is that he is relevant not as a new version of psychology that may improve the discipline, as some sympathetic writers would have it, but as an *alternative* to psychology; as far as Lacan (1975/1991: 278) was concerned, 'psychology is itself an error of perspective on the human being'. Lacanian psychoanalysis provides a series of theoretical frameworks, not a single closed system, that help us to think in an entirely different way about what are usually taken to be 'psychological' phenomena.

This is important for two reasons. First, each attempt to make Lacan's work compatible with traditional academic psychology necessarily entails a particular kind of distortion of his work. Although a brief review of Lacan's work focused on one problematic, such as this, may render his often cryptic writing and transcribed public seminars more accessible, that accessibility produces a loss of meaning at the very same moment that it appears to facilitate understanding. The immediate impression that one 'understands' an argument, a text or another person lies, in Lacanian terms, on an 'imaginary' axis governed by processes of mirroring in which we recognize or, more to the point, 'misrecognize' that which we have already expected to see there, that which owes more to what we ourselves are than what is other to us (Lacan, 1949). Second, Lacan's teaching and writing were bound up with a practice of analysis that was concerned with questioning the truth claims of psychological experts and the attempts, evident in the endeavour of dominant tendencies in US psychoanalysis, to adapt individuals to society. Lacan's (1953: 38) argument, that 'the conception of psychoanalysis in the United States has inclined towards the adaptation of the individual to the social environment, towards the quest for behaviour patterns, and towards all the objectification implied in the notion of "human engineering"', would seem to be relevant at least as much to Western psychology as to ostensibly 'psychoanalytic' ego-psychology (Ingleby, 1985).

Both 'understanding' and 'adaptation', then, are anathema to Lacan, and each needs to be questioned and rethought. Lacan was not, nor should he be thought of as, a psychologist. Towards the end of the chapter I will make the case that he would be better characterized as a 'barred psychologist', and that what he offers to psychology, if anything, is something that helps us to unravel and reflect upon the assumptions psychologists make about who they are and what they do. What psychologists do is structured by a system of theories and practices, and what coherence there is to psychology is given by this system as a disciplinary apparatus (Rose, 1985). To many of those about to be recruited into it, this disciplinary apparatus first manifests as a 'syllabus'. So this chapter addresses different areas of psychology that comprise the core syllabus for undergraduates in the English-speaking world and then turns to more general conceptions of the individual before reviewing the implications of a different kind of engagement by psychologists with Lacan's work.

Individual cognitive psychology

Mainstream Anglo-American psychology (in which the agenda is largely set by US texts and journals and which has a profound influence in shaping the discipline throughout the English-speaking world) is now underpinned by a model of the individual as 'information-processor' (Lindsay and Norman, 1972). A reaction against Pavlovian and Watsonian behaviourism in the 1950s, which tended to deny the relevance of internal mental states, led to the development of 'cognitive science', and investigation of problem-solving and memory governed by at least implicit, and often explicit, computational metaphors (Winograd and Flores, 1987). This shift of focus, designed to capture processes happening inside the head, has increasingly defined what psychology should be. Even alternative approaches, such as Skinnerian radical behaviourism and descriptions of cognition as modularized and distributed, have operated with reference to the information-processing model (Fodor, 1983).

Psychoanalysts would recognize this model as a version of 'ego-psychology' (e.g. Hartmann, 1939/1958), for there are strong assumptions here about the independent existence of central command processes that are studied *as if* they operate in an integrated way even while notions of skill, error, faulty functioning and incomplete heuristics always accompany the model. Psychological studies of intelligence, personality and social skills then take this model as given, and they typically issue in recommendations for cognitive behavioural treatments for inadequate functioning (e.g. Trower *et al.*, 1978). Here psychology adopts a Cartesian dualist view of a necessary division between thinking and the body in which reason is viewed as operating from a single point of certainty beset, as a condition for its own pre-eminence, by doubt. Lacan's work throws this cognitivist model of the individual into question on a number of counts, of which we may briefly note four here.

Thinking in language

First, thinking is understood by Lacan to be something operating within language, and so as an activity that is public and social rather than private and individual. For Lacan (1981/1993: 112), '*thought* means the thing articulated in language'. This means that it would be misplaced to investigate 'thought' as something occurring inside the head as if it were then necessarily outside language, and a Lacanian understanding of thinking in language also entails a rejection of notions of 'communication' as the transmission of thoughts from one head to another through a transparent medium, with language assumed to be such a medium (Shannon and Weaver, 1949). The formal structure of language itself also constitutes the content of the communication, through internal relations that operate independently of the subject. It would be possible, by way of this focus on shared social processes, to connect Lacan here with work on 'practical cognition' drawing on Russian activity theory and US ethnomethodology (e.g. Lave, 1988). In this way, it may seem as if it were possible to build a bridge across to Lacan.

However, what is missing from this work is any account of the unconscious, which for Lacanian work as a form of psychoanalysis, of course, is crucial. For Lacan, however, the unconscious is not equivalent to 'non-conscious' thought that is prevented by various cognitively conceived 'defence mechanisms' from coming into awareness. The unconscious is produced when the infant enters language as the structured domain of meaning that lies beyond our grasp as individuals. This language, which alienates us at the very same moment that it creates a channel of communication with others, comprises 'signifiers' structured into discourse, into a symbolic realm. This is what Lacan refers to as the 'symbolic order', and so the symbolic order determines the sense that is given to our words and the sense of lack that arises from our failure to master it. The symbolic order is always 'other' to us, and so a Lacanian conception of the unconscious is of it as the 'discourse of the Other'; it is a relay of desire and site of individual cognitive 'accomplishments' (to use an ethnomethodological term) as well as communicational activity. A shift to 'practical cognition' (Lave, 1988) is not sufficient to account for the role of the symbolic order and its effect in the human subject as the domain of the unconscious. In this respect, Lacan's account of 'cognition' in relation to language is completely at odds with anything recognizably psychological.

Meaning and memory

Second, there is a shift from questions of mechanism to questions of *meaning*. Here, Lacan sometimes employs a phenomenological description of the ways in which things in the world mean something to the subject. This is the point in his early writings where he elaborates a view of the human being and its relation to 'Being' that is very close to Heidegger (1928/1962), and which thus makes plausible a comparison with hermeneutics in psychology (Packer, 1985). However, this Heideggerian account of 'Being-in-the-world' is supplemented by Lacan, transformed theoretically, and so ineluctably overturned. As Lacan (1981/1993: 104) puts it, 'remembering necessarily takes place within the symbolic order'. The symbolic order does provide a space or, in Heideggerian terms, a 'clearing' for the subject, but the organization of signifiers is out of the grasp of the subject, and these signifiers within the discourse of the Other – as unconscious – determine how the subject will come to be and the sense that they have that they are always lacking something. For Lacan (1981/1993: 111), 'a recollection – that is, a resurgence of an impression – is organized in historical continuity'.

One implication of this can be seen in the radically different way Lacan accounts for *déjà vu*. Cognitive explanations appeal to physiological accounts of delays in neuronal pathways, for example, to explain why people sometimes have the experience of seeing things already seen, but for Lacan (1981/1993: 112),

> *Déjà vu* occurs when a situation is lived through with a full symbolic meaning which reproduces a homologous symbolic situation that has been previously lived through but forgotten, and which is lived through again without the subject's understanding it in all its detail. This is what gives the subject the impression that he has already seen the context, the scene, of the present moment.

Although a phenomenological account often seems to be evoked in Lacan's work, then, the *symbolic* organization of memory makes that experience of 'meaning' something quite different, something that must obey the logic of the signifier. To treat 'meaning' as self-sufficient and independent of the *symbolic* would be to render it, in Lacanian terms, as an *imaginary* order of experience. This imaginary realm that gives us the sense of 'understanding' and 'communication' is very important, but Lacan's description of the unconscious as discourse of the Other in the realm of the symbolic order reveals this imaginary domain as illusory and so as a quite mistaken ground upon which to construct any scientific account of what the human subject is and how it came to be. The phenomenon of 'memory', then, is another of those 'cognitive' phenomena that are *outside* the subject, and so it is not amenable to 'psychological' investigation.

Cogito and body

Third, Lacan displaces the Cartesian *cogito* in such a way that thinking and being are seen as operating in relation to one another but not from the same point. He explicitly challenges the presumption of cognitive psychology that an understanding of the nature of human thinking is also an insight into what it is to be a human being. One of his formulations of the relationship between thinking and being, then, is 'I think where I am not therefore I am where I do not think' (Lacan, 1957: 166). The human subject is seen as split, as 'barred' from any full presence or self-identity, and this split subject is rendered by Lacan by means of the figure 'S̷', the 'barred subject'. This divided nature of subjectivity raises two problems for cognitive psychology to do with mental activity that lies outside consciousness and with the body.

Lacan reinterprets 'Being' as described by Heidegger (1928/1962) as the unconscious in the field of the Other, and from this reinterpretation he develops an account of 'thinking' as not separable from the body, but as always proceeding through symbolic activity. The use of Heideggerian reflections on the human being in relation to 'Being', particularly evident in Lacan's early work, gives rise to an account of subjectivity as decentred from the place where thinking is usually assumed to operate in cognitive accounts, but also an account of it as embodied (Richardson, 1980). It would then be possible to connect such an embodied conception of thinking with critiques of cognitive psychology from within philosophy that have taken as their prime target work on 'artificial intelligence' (AI). Heidegger (1928/1962) has been an important influence in such work, for example in the claim that computers would need bodies in order to be able to be correctly ascribed with 'intelligence' (Dreyfus, 1967). What differentiates Lacan from these critiques, however, is his reinterpretation of the relation between the body and 'Being'. And to turn from mainstream AI to 'embodiment' will not solve the problem, because for Lacan the body too is radically 'decentred' from the subject.

Rather than the body being a site of 'Being' where thinking really takes place, however, it is seen as the 'real' basis through which symbolic activity must pass (Soler, 1995). For Lacan, then, there is always a complex interimplication of the three orders of the 'symbolic', the 'imaginary' and the 'real'. It is the embodied characteristic of thinking through the body as mediator in the field of the Other as unconscious that makes it possible for the human being to have 'symptoms'. Conversion hysteria, for example, occurs when bits of the body are turned into signifiers – the classic symptoms in psychoanalytic case histories – and the human subject speaks through them because he or she has been unable to speak otherwise. The place of 'cognitive' activity as understood by cognitive psychology is thus displaced from the point where psychologists expect it to be or would be able to describe it within their theoretical frameworks.

Cognition and symptom

Fourth, the ego for Lacan is not assumed to provide a privileged point from which the subject surveys his or her body and soul, and there is no 'conflict-free sphere' of the ego as described, for example, by the ego-psychologists that might make such a vantage point possible. Here ego-psychology converges with descriptions of sensation and perception assumed to provide the bedrock of cognitive psychology, but Lacan diametrically opposes such assumptions. Rather than being taken for granted, the image of the ego as an objective point of access to consciousness and relationships is something dubious to be inspected, subjected to close analysis. For Lacan (1975/1991: 16),

> every advance made by this ego psychology can be summed up as follows – the ego is structured exactly like a symptom. At the heart of the matter, it is only a privileged symptom, the human symptom *par excellence,* the mental illness of man.

To claim that the ego is a 'symptom' is to invite an explanation and interpretation of how it has come to be crystallized in the psychic economy of the subject.

Psychological models of 'cognition' are predicated on culturally specific images of telephone-exchange wiring connections, office filing systems and, now increasingly, computer disk-management, and on an experiential resonance between these activities and the sense of self and thinking elaborated for subjects in Western culture. These models are themselves expressions *of* something psychopathological in everyday life and they communicate, albeit in distorted ways, something of the peculiarity of contemporary subjectivity, rather than being an accurate rendition of what lies inside the head, under the surface of observable behaviour (Parker, 1997b). It is in that sense that they can be said to be 'symptomatic', and thus what cognitive psychology takes as its starting point Lacan sees as part of the problem.

While it would be convenient to assume that this radical opposition to cognitive accounts of mental phenomena leads Lacan into a simple rapprochement with radical behaviourism, the social construction of subjectivity in language that his account entails is dialectically if not diametrically opposed to behaviourism (a question I explore in Chapter 3 of this book). Lacan does not just substitute an attention to external forces for internal mechanisms, as can be seen if we turn to approaches in psychology that have concerned themselves with the external world and with the importance of social relationships in human experience.

Developmental and social psychology

Contrasts between psychological accounts of cognitive processes and Lacanian re-descriptions of them would seem at first glance simply to lead us
to shift 'Lacan as psychologist' from the domain of 'core' individual psychology into the realm of developmental and social psychology. Lacanian
accounts of 'cognition' seem to call for a developmental and social sensitivity that mainstream individual psychology lacks, but Lacan did not provide
a 'developmental psychological' or 'social psychological' account either.

Developmental psychology

Sometimes Lacan's (1949/1977a) account of the 'mirror stage' – in which
the infant, at about eighteen months of age, takes the image of an Other,
perhaps in a real mirror, as the 'imaginary' model for its own self – is set
alongside other developmental accounts as if it functioned as an improve-
ment, as if it told the 'real' story about how the child comes to imagine its
body and ready itself for the entry into language (e.g. Frosh, 1989). However, although the discrete elements of Lacan's description can be separated
out and linked with empirical studies in psychology (e.g. Muller, 1996),
things are very different when this 'stage', which is not really a stage at all,
is seen in the context of a Lacanian account of the history of the individual
subject.

Developmental psychology rests on the assumption that the passage from
infancy to adulthood is governed by a maturational sequence that can be
discovered empirically and then delimited theoretically (Burman, 2008a).
The dominant view of this sequence is expressed in the hope that normative
'ages and stages' of development can be identified so that developmental
delays due to failures in biological hard-wiring or inadequate parenting can
be understood and perhaps rectified (e.g. Mitchell, 1992). Piagetian descriptions of the development of cognitive structures, which are augmented by
schemas for moral development in Kohlberg's work, are more sophisticated,
arguing, for example, that the sequence rests more on the logical emergence
of structures for which 'earlier' structures are prerequisite than the simple
unfolding of age-specific stages, and these descriptions have invited comparison with Lacan's work (Silverman, 1980).

Vygotskyan accounts of the development of thinking through language
seem to break even more radically from US developmental psychology,
and by virtue of that, perhaps, seem to come closer to Lacanian conceptions (Walkerdine, 1982). However, although Lacan's account of 'development' does appeal to a logical account, the logic is not *sequential*. It is not
even 'developmental' in the sense that psychologists would understand the

term, for any memory of the emergence of the subject in language that may be thought of as logically prerequisite is itself constituted *after* the event, as a supplement to the experience that then has the effect of changing it. Here Lacan retrieves Freud's account of the memory of trauma as operating *nachträglich* (as 'retroactive'), and he does this in order to respecify the nature of development as happening at each turn after a developmental psychologist could ever observe it. Lacanian analytic training does not include infant observation partly for this reason, for the relation between the mother and baby and the impact of events in the infant's childhood are not things that one could ever see in their natural unmediated state (cf. Miller *et al.*, 1989).

Lacan (1981/1993: 7) set himself against psychologically grounded versions of psychoanalysis as well as psychology itself in his comment, for example, that 'the great secret of psychoanalysis is that there is no psychogenesis'. The temporal relation between past and present is something that is constructed and reconstructed by the subject in ways that will defeat any developmental account that tries to define how particular events in the past will have psychological sequelae:

> What is realized in my history is not the past definite of what was, since it is no more, or even the present perfect of what has been in what I am, but the future anterior of what I shall have been for what I am in the process of becoming.
>
> (Lacan, 1956/1977b: 86)

The way that human subjects reflect upon their 'past' (as if it were 'the past definite'), then, will, at that moment, transform it into something that anticipates the present (into 'what shall have been'), and it is the *relation* subjects have with their past and whatever traumatic events may have actually transpired that will block or facilitate what they may experience as their 'development' (their 'process of becoming').

Although contemporary developmental psychology does try to address the development of the infant in relation to others, it still does so through trying to capture the nature of particular interactions, usually between the infant and the mother (e.g. Muller, 1996). Lacan's account of otherness, in contrast, grounds 'development' in relation to the mother not as such but as Other. The relation between the infant and the mother is, according to Lacan, governed by 'imaginary' mirroring, but that relation is, in turn, governed by symbolic processes that lie out of the control of infant or mother. Those symbolic processes lie within the domain of signifiers that give meaning to the relationship, and this symbolic order operates as 'Other'. Lacan (1975/1998) attempted to formalize theoretical descriptions of clinical phenomena so that they could be 'transmissible' as 'mathemes'. In this case, individual subjectivity is constituted in relation to the Other, represented by the matheme 'A' (for *Autre*, French for 'Other'), and the processes of alienation and separation give rise to a fantasy of the Other as always incomplete (Lacan, 1964/1973). The matheme for the barred subject ('$') , then, is always in relation to the Other, but the infant cannot establish a direct unmediated relationship with that Other, and so the longed-for fullness of being that the Other represents is experienced as lacking. Just as the subject is barred from full self-presence, divided against itself, so the Other is also barred (A̶). It functions, then, as an Other that always fails, always lacks what was expected of it. The human subject is always in relation to others, then, and this makes 'developmental' accounts of the emerging 'psychology' of individual subjects very difficult. For Lacanians, perhaps, it makes such accounts impossible.

Social psychology

It may be inferred from this account, then, that developmental psychology should become more 'social', and that social psychology would be the place in the discipline where Lacan might find a natural home. But this is not so. Social psychology assumes a separation between the individual and the social, and when it prioritizes social processes or 'group processes' over the activities of the individual it still leaves the relation between the two sides unexamined (Henriques *et al.*, 1984/1998; Parker, 1989). The dichotomous *relation* between the individual and the social is then mapped onto the opposition between the 'inside' of the subject and the 'outside'. The attempt to provide fully social explanations of human behaviour in social psychology has been bedevilled by the reduction of explanation to the level of the individual, and the individual–social dichotomy has also structured the various attempts to describe conflict and aggression in the discipline that drew on psychoanalytic concepts (Billig, 1976).

When psychoanalysis is brought into the equation, and the equation itself is left intact, this leads to a conception of an 'inside' and an 'outside' in which the unconscious is treated as a domain outside language, and as something that operates at the level of the individual, inside the mind. Against this conception, in Lacan's work the complex relationship between conscious and unconscious and between inside and outside disturbs that equation; one way Lacan (1964/1973) evokes that relationship is through the figure of the 'Möbius strip', in which the outside of the band folds around and turns into the inside rather than there being a definable distinct break between the two realms. Lacan uses the motif of the Möbius strip not only because it displays a different relationship between the inside (usually assumed to be the realm of the unconscious) and the outside, but also because it draws attention to a *temporal* relationship between the two that is at least as important as, if not more so than, the spatial relationship. For Lacan, then, the unconscious is at least as much 'outside' as 'inside'; and 'it is the closing of the unconscious which provides the key to its space – namely the impropriety of trying to turn it into an inside' (Lacan, 1966: 267). Because social psychology rests upon an image of individuals existing in social space and interacting with other people in that space, it cannot assimilate a Lacanian view of each individual human subject as always already social. Lacanian 'psychology', then, is not 'social psychology'.

Methodological alternatives in psychology

Lacan may not sit easily with mainstream approaches in the discipline, but there have been a number of innovations that may be expected to operate as a convenient interface. Alternative traditions of work inside psychology in recent years have tended to develop more on the ground of methodology than through the development of substantive theoretical models. It could be argued that this is not surprising, for the discipline of psychology has actually been historically defined more by method than by theory, and its primary function as part of the 'psychological complex' was and is as a regulative apparatus for observing, categorizing and adapting individuals to the social (Rose, 1985). Humanist 'new paradigm' and 'social construction-ist' approaches, for example, even when they have advanced new models, have emphasized how research should be carried out, and they have either elaborated accounts of morally accountable individuals from that base (e.g. Harré and Secord, 1972; Reason and Rowan, 1981) or been wary of defining once and for all what human beings are like (e.g. Burr, 2003; Gergen, 1985). But Lacan is neither a humanistic psychologist nor a social constructionist.

Humanism

Lacan was deeply influenced by phenomenology but he was not a phenom-enologist, still less a humanist, and still less so a humanistic psychologist. A Lacanian view of subjectivity is very different from that of the human-ists, for whom there is an assumption that communication can be rendered completely open, and so individual motivations may be made transparent to the subject and others (Parker, 1999b). Instead, the role of subjectivity in the discipline is brought to the fore by the argument that 'in psychology, objectification is subjected in its very principle to a law of *méconnaissance* [misrecognition] that governs the subject not only as observed, but also as observer' (Lacan, 1956: 130). Lacan is not calling for a more genuine relationship between observers and observed in psychological research here, and his attention to subjectivity is driven by a concern with 'ethics' that is quite different from the notions of transparency and holistic understanding that drive contemporary qualitative research (Lacan, 1986). Transparency of communication is a worthwhile ideal, perhaps, but for Lacan this lies on the axis of the 'imaginary', and we need a more radical approach to grasp how our understanding is always structured by the symbolic order. And while we may want to establish a direct, unmediated relationship between ourselves and those whom we observe, Lacan's argument that we ourselves are barred subjects ('$), divided by virtue of being human beings who use language and incapable of unmediated understanding of ourselves, would throw into question that idealized image of the researcher–researched relationship.

The problem with psychological investigation, for Lacan, lies not in its dehumanizing of subjects *per se* but in positivist procedures that mislead us about the nature and place of the phenomena psychologists wish to understand. We can take as an example of this the activity of the detectives in Lacan's commentary on Edgar Allen Poe's tale 'The Purloined Letter' (1844/1938; see Plon, 1974). The detectives search for a stolen letter in the apartment of a government minister whom they know to be concealing it, and they search in such minute detail, with such an obsessive focus on the hidden object, that they cannot see that it is right in front of their eyes. Lacan (1956/1972: 54–55) points out that 'the detectives have so immutable a notion of the real that they fail to notice that their search tends to transform it into its object'. Again, he is drawing attention to the role of the symbolic order in structuring how we understand the world and understand ourselves, and such an attention cannot be obtained through a simple recourse to humanistic psychology.

Social constructionism

Lacan was not against science, reason or truth. For that reason it would be a mistake to see him as a 'post-structuralist', which is an Anglo-American category that draws disparate writers together under a rubric without much sense in France when Lacan was writing, and still less as an adherent of 'postmodernism', which appeals to a supposed historical mutation in contemporary culture to warrant a flight from any grand narrative of personal, social or scientific understanding (Gergen, 1991). Lacan (1981/1993: 143) notes that 'it's the starting point of modern science not to trust the phenomena and to look for something more subsistent behind them that explains them', and so 'our way of proceeding is scientific'.

In some respects, Lacanian objections to the notion of separate enclosed cognition seem close to recent descriptions of 'collective remembering' in the broad social constructionist tradition (Gergen, 1985). Lacan's argument that memory is bound up with the subject's place in language anticipates some of the work on collective memory informed by activity theory, ethnomethodology and 'discursive psychology' (Middleton and Edwards, 1990). The argument that mental processes take place in and through language is not, in itself, so strange to some contemporary 'discourse analysts' (e.g. Parker, 1992, 2002), and mainstream psychologists could claim that Lacan simply belongs with discourse analysis as part of that particular methodological alternative in the discipline (cf. Parker, 1997a).

However, the apparent connection between dominant tendencies in recent discursive psychology such as conversation analysis, which traces the moment-by-moment activity of turn-taking and construction of sense between participants in everyday interaction, and Lacanian views of discourse would involve a misunderstanding of how Lacan sees language working. For Lacan (1966/1995: 267), it is necessary to attend to 'the retroactive effect of meaning in sentences, meaning requiring the last word of a sentence to be sealed'. This means that detailed analysis of transcripts that attend to turn-taking or the functions of various rhetorical forms (e.g. Potter, 1996) will take a methodological stance that adopts commonsensical notions of cause and effect reconfigured through 'stake' and 'function'. The eschewal of theory in conversation-analytic versions of discursive psychology also betrays the promise often made by its practitioners to give a critical account of discourse and the place of psychology within it (cf. Parker, 2001). In addition, at the very moment the conversation analysts obey the empiricist demands made by psychologists to conform to their version of what scientific inquiry looks like, they *fail* to address the character of the subject in relation to the signifier theoretically specified by Lacan.

Psychology and anti-psychology

Lacanian concepts are difficult to capture and define not only because Lacan himself is notoriously difficult to read, but also because the concepts are always *relational*. The sense in which it is true to say that Lacan is 'structuralist' lies in the way in which elements of his theoretical interventions and clinical categories themselves can only be understood in terms of their changing relations with the other elements. With respect to psychological concepts, then, Lacan relentlessly *de-substantializes* phenomena that are usually reified by the discipline, that are usually rendered as if they were observable and empirically verifiable things.

This can be illustrated by the notion of the *objet petit a*, and the difference between its status as an 'object' of desire and the way an 'object' is usually conceived of in psychoanalytic object-relations theory (e.g. Greenberg and Mitchell, 1983). Object-relations theory supposes that the objects and 'part objects' of the infant's phenomenal world are either representations of real things (objects and subjects) in the external world or representations of instincts. Lacan's notion of the object as *objet petit a*, however, is a radically different concept. Rather than something that can be simply equated with the mother, father, penis or faeces, its status in Lacan's work is simultaneously as 'lost object' and object cause of desire. While object-relations theory looks to empirical studies in developmental psychology to confirm its already psychologized descriptions of internal mental functioning (e.g. Stern, 1985; cf. Cushman, 1991), Lacan's relentless de-substantializing of the object in the contrasting overlapping uses of *objet petit a* resists any such appeal to psychology.

For Lacan (1964/1973: 270), the *objet petit a* is constituted for the subject as object cause of desire as something (fantasized as some thing), which becomes operative at the very moment that it is lost: '*a* fills the gap constituted by the inaugural division of the subject.' The '*a*' fascinates us because it holds the promise of that ideal object that we come to believe that we once possessed and that forever escapes our grasp. It is constituted by the subject as that thing that shines for him or her only from a specific position, and Lacan (1964/1973) elaborates this idea using the metaphor of 'anamorphosis' in painting, in which a smear or meaningless figure only becomes decipherable from a certain viewpoint (as in the image of the skull in Holbein's painting *The Ambassadors*). Not only is the *objet petit a* precisely not amenable to be rendered as a thing (and in the nearest to it being so, as a fetish, it would lose its character as *objet petit a*), but it comes into being as an element only in a particular subject's fantasy structure.

It has been pointed out that

> few of Lacan's concepts have so many avatars in Lacan's work: the other, *agalma*, the golden number, the Freudian thing, the real, the anomaly, the cause of desire, surplus jouissance, the materiality of language, the analyst's desire, logical consistency, the Other's desire, semblance/sham, the lost object, and so on and so forth.
>
> (Fink, 1995: 83)

The very *indeterminacy* of *objet petit a* is one of its theoretical strengths, and that indeterminacy gives it a function within Lacan's work that is, for his readers, uncannily like an *objet petit a* itself. Theoretical concepts that function in this kind of way are anathema to the discipline of psychology, and it is important that psychologists who may be attracted to Lacan's work recognize this.

Barred psychology

Asking how psychologists may be able to approach Lacan and adopt him as a lost psychologist is to pose the wrong question. Lacan himself conducted a sarcastic and vituperative campaign against psychoanalysts who wanted to 'psychologize' Freud's work. In part, this was because the distortions of psychoanalysis wrought by US ego-psychologists were designed to render their clinical practice as something more 'scientific' and closer to medicine. Lacan argued that the attempt to adapt the individual to society in mainstream psychoanalysis after the Second World War through the identification of the patient's ego with that of the analyst was a process that expressed and reproduced the attempt by Central European *émigré* analysts themselves to adapt to the more conservative and medicalized institutions they encountered upon their arrival in the United States (cf. Jacoby, 1983). For Lacan, this was a betrayal of what was most subversive about psychoanalysis.

In part, Lacan's express hostility to psychology was due to his betrayal by those who chose to ally with the International Psychoanalytic Association (IPA) against him when he was eventually excluded from the function of training analyst in that organization in 1963. The attempt to render Lacan's reading of Freud comprehensible to psychoanalysts working with what were essentially psychological assumptions about empirically verifiable ego development and images of healthy ego functioning led even some of those sympathetic to him eventually to adopt formulations that were acceptable to the IPA analysts in Chicago and New York and to academic psychology in Paris (Roudinesco, 1990). The importance of the institutional location of psychoanalysis *outside* the 'discourse of the university' became increasingly coupled by Lacan (1991/2007) with the independence of psychoanalysis from psychology as such. The key question, then, was how to defend psychoanalysis from the kinds of distortions that a psychological understanding of behaviour would inflict rather than attempt to take psychological curiosity about psychoanalysis on good coin.

This does not mean that Lacanians will rule out of court each and every phenomenon described by psychologists. Lacan's (2006) own account of the 'mirror stage' draws upon work by United States-based child psychoanalysts (Bühler's descriptions of 'transitivism' as intense behavioural mimetic identification between infants), by animal ethologists (descriptions of the importance of the image of other members of the species for social behaviour and sexual maturation in locusts and pigeons) and by Gestalt psychologists (Köhler's description of jubilant recognition in monkeys during their perception of situations and relations between things).

The descriptions by the Gestalt psychologist Zeigarnik of the effects of unfinished tasks upon later activity are also offered by Lacanians, for example, as a warrant for ending analytic sessions early; the patient will then be more likely to ponder on the material and resume work on it in the following session (Burgoyne, 1997). Lacan and Lacanian psychoanalysts may well draw upon work by psychologists to develop and illustrate theory and practice in their own distinct domain of work. With respect to the Zeigarnik effect, introduced by a psychologist and psychoanalyst, Daniel Lagache, to account for the phenomenon of transference, for example, Lacan was very cautious. After damning Lagache with faint praise for introducing 'an idea which was bound to please at a time when psychoanalysis seemed to be short of alibis' (Lacan, 1952: 62), he made it clear that the Zeigarnik effect *depends* upon transference rather than explaining it.

It is now possible to move to a formulation of Lacan's relationship with psychology that characterizes his work by way of a matheme. The *objet petit a* (represented as 'a') and the barred subject (represented as 'S') are mathemes, and can be combined to represent psychoanalytic concepts like fantasy (in which '$S \lozenge a$' serves as the matheme to capture the barred subject's relation to the object). It could be said that Lacanian psychoanalysis operates in relation to some critical psychologists now looking for new theoretical frameworks as an *objet petit a*, and for them it can be an object cause of desire that is kept at a distance by psychology and is, for that very reason perhaps, all the more fascinating.

The problem for psychology is that Lacanian psychoanalysis does not yield the kind of understanding that many of those psychologists who have discovered it desire. Lacan himself is, then, perhaps best characterized as someone who operates as the antithesis of psychology, as well as being excluded from the mainstream psychoanalytic establishment, by the matheme for a 'barred psychologist' (Ψ). Lacan is a barred psychologist not only because he has been barred from the discipline so far, and his work is deliberately set against the rules of the game that psychologists follow in their version of scientific inquiry. He also presents theoretical accounts that seem designed to prohibit understanding on the part of psychologists. Sometimes his accounts are filtered in such a way as to make it seem as if they can be understood psychologically, but as we look more closely at his writings we find ourselves barred from entering them if we maintain our identity as psychologists.

Conclusions

The stakes may be summarized dialectically, in an appropriately paradoxical way, as follows. If Lacan is treated as a 'psychologist' and his work is seen as amenable to re-description as a form of psychology, then psychologists will have gained nothing by engaging with him. The illusion of understanding will be as a form of 'false connection' that not only adapts Lacan to a discipline he scorned, but that also continues the adaptation of individuals to the existing social order, an enterprise he condemned, when it was attempted by the ego-psychologists, as little better than 'orthopaedics' (Lacan, 1964/1973: 23). He reiterated the point time and again that psychoanalytic experience is 'irreducible to all psychology considered as the objectification of certain properties of the individual' (Lacan, 1952: 62).

It has only been through theoretical work entirely conceptually independent of the assumptions that psychologists make about the human subject that Lacanians have been able to accumulate a corpus of material that may now operate as an alternative pole of attraction for psychologists disenchanted with what their own discipline has to offer. Now, while IPA analysts may look to the discipline of psychology to confirm their image of the individual and to validate certain forms of treatment, Lacanian psychoanalysts need to emphasize that Lacan provides something completely different, something that is not, and should not be tempted to become, psychology.

The consequences of this account of Lacan's work in relation to psychology are wide-ranging. Apart from issues of scholarship, which this call for an accurate reading of his work entails, there are implications for clinical practice and the extent to which clinical psychologists and Lacanian psychoanalysts may be tempted to distort their work to fit a mistaken image of the human subject because that is the image that is sanctioned by present-day psychology (cf. Fink, 1997). Lacanian psychoanalysis is necessarily also a critique of received wisdoms about the self, and in this respect it is also important to know what Lacan actually said if there is to be a serious assessment of his contribution to 'critical' perspectives in psychology (Fox and Prilleltensky, 1997; Parker, 2000). If Lacan is read as a 'barred psychologist' ($\not\Psi$), someone who relentlessly disrupts what psychologists think they know, then his work may provoke a reinterpretation that constructs a space for work inside psychology that revolves around the questions he asked about the nature of the human subject, rather than answers that usually function to foreclose further inquiry.

2 Lacan, psychology and the discourse of the university

This chapter focuses on the quite specific context of the way psychology is taught, and so the argument chimes with critical psychological perspectives in the discipline. There is always a danger that psychoanalysis might be read as a set of empirical phenomena or as an alternative paradigm that might remedy and replace mainstream psychology. We saw in the last chapter that Lacan disturbs that view of psychoanalysis. This is important because psychoanalysis has a long-standing relationship with psychology (even though the historical connections between the two domains of study are often obscured in psychology textbooks) and psychoanalysis now is attractive to some 'psychosocial' critical psychologists because it offers quite different understandings of subjectivity.

It will become clear that this chapter is written from a standpoint which draws upon psychoanalysis only insofar as it disrupts the certainties of mainstream psychology and it treats psychoanalysis as a discursive phenomenon. Lacanian psychoanalysis here is also being reconfigured as something that is in some sense a 'social construction'. I describe and utilize Lacan's account of the 'discourse of the university' and you will see the relevance of this to the operation of psychological discourse in academic institutions.

The chapter develops the argument Lacan makes in his 1969–1970 Seminar 'The Reverse of Psychoanalysis' (Lacan, 2007) in order to bring psychoanalysis to bear on psychology as a critical conceptual tool, not as a full-blown paradigmatic alternative. The Lacanian notions of 'knowledge as a battery of signifiers', 'master signifier', '*objet petit a*' and 'barred subject' in the four positions of the discourse he describes (of agent, other, truth and product) are used to interpret the operation of psychology from a critical standpoint. Attention is drawn to the 'bar' between agent and truth and between other and product, and I also draw out implications for the existing humanist critiques of psychology.

Social constructionist perspectives have been very useful in recent years in helping us see that the kind of things psychologists study are created in the very process of identifying them (Burr, 2003; Gergen, 1999). We can now step back and focus on the way mental states and behavioural processes are 'storied into being' (Curt, 1994). The social constructionist movement in psychology shifts our attention to the narratives that show us psychological phenomena, and we see the work that those narratives do rather than assuming that we are accessing the things themselves. Discourse analysis has provided detailed studies of the way that psychology constitutes certain kinds of object, actually many kinds of object ranging from cognitive mechanisms to personality types (Potter and Wetherell, 1987; Edwards, 1992), and some forms of discourse analysis have also drawn on the work of Michel Foucault to examine how certain forms of *subject* are constituted by psychological discourse (Parker, 1992). This is why some critical psychologists have been attracted to Foucault's writing (Parker, 1999a).

Psychology works because the people who are studied by academic psychologists, and who are the objects of the practice of professional psychologists, are made and remake themselves as psychological subjects, those kind of subjects who really do experience themselves as having A-type personalities or prejudices or unconscious defence mechanisms. The Foucauldian strand of discourse analysis has been particularly important in showing how the discursive constitution of psychological objects and subjects is always set against a background of historically sedimented forms of talk and writing and all of the other practices ranging from architecture to artistic representation that make up the discourses that bear us (Burman *et al.*, 1996; Parker and the Bolton Discourse Network, 1999). These 'conditions of possibility' mean that certain kinds of things make sense to be storied into being and other kinds of things are consigned to the realms of madness. The broad historical conditions of possibility are the location for specific practices where new forms of discourse are elaborated; in Foucauldian jargon the 'surfaces of emergence'. The psy-complex as a web of theories and practices to do with the mind and behaviour and how they may be governed contains many surfaces of emergence for the recombination of old ideas and the production of new ones (Ingleby, 1985; Rose, 1985). Psychological journals are one such site, and the rules that govern them determine what can be written and said and how we write and read things, and absorb or dismiss them.

Foucault (1980) is an excellent resource for displaying the links between discourse and knowledge and identifying the role of psychology as a discipline in instituting certain 'regimes of truth' so that psychologists know what they know about other people. He shows how psychologists subscribe to an epistemology in which they can study others as if they were objects without reflecting on the otherness of those they study or the otherness of themselves to their objects, the subjects. But we can go further than this by making use of another rather surprising theoretical resource, another theorist of discourse who had critical things to say about psychology: Lacan. As a psychiatrist and psychoanalyst he was heavily implicated in the proliferating disciplinary and confessional apparatuses that comprise the psy-complex (Macey, 1988). That makes him a risky resource for those who want to distance themselves from mainstream psychology, and some writers on discursive psychology and psychoanalysis are attracted to Freud but repelled by Lacan, for understandable reasons (Billig, 1999; cf. Parker, 2001). Nevertheless, Lacan holds a fascination for some critical psychologists because he seems to offer an alternative way of understanding subjectivity. That psychoanalytic subjectivity is not what concerns me here (see Parker, 2000). What I want to do instead is to argue that Lacan is an even better resource than many critical psychologists suspect, but not because he gives us a better kind of psychology. Precisely the reverse.

The reverse of psychology

Lacan's theoretical interventions were as much directed against psychology as against distortions of psychoanalysis itself. These distortions were, for Lacan, incarnate in the International Psychoanalytic Association (IPA) and found their quintessential expression in the development in the United States of 'ego-psychology'. Ego-psychology (e.g. Hartmann, 1939/1958) entailed a rapprochement with mainstream academic psychology and the adoption of descriptions of personality development that had hitherto been anathema to psychoanalysis.

Lacan objected to psychology for two main reasons. First, conceptually, because ego-psychology pursued the aim of adaptation of the subject to society through the elaboration of a model of the 'individual' which is amenable to what he termed an 'orthopaedics' (Lacan, 1964/1973). This is an endeavour that is mechanistic and reductive, and as such intensely problematic. Second, historically, because the emergence of a distinct Lacanian tradition entailed a break in 1963 which separated what was to become the EFP (*École freudienne de Paris*) from those willing to sacrifice Lacan in exchange for IPA recognition, including, significantly for Lacan, the psychologist and university academic Daniel Lagache (Roudinesco, 1990). The avowed 'return to Freud' in Lacan's work was not intended to take literally each and every contradictory proposition in Freud's writing – and Lacan himself voices disagreements with Freud – but to read Freud psychoanalytically rather than psychologistically. An important part of the Lacanian tradition's work revolves around a distinctive understanding of discourse and the operation of different discourses in contemporary culture.

Lacan's (1991/2007) description of four discourses provides a way of distinguishing forms of symbolic social bond and positions for the subject. Here I want to focus specifically on the 'discourse of the university'. The other discourses Lacan describes are the 'discourse of the master', the 'discourse of the hysteric' and the 'discourse of the analyst'. Lacan's account is in Seminar XVII, *L'envers de la psychanalyse*, the 'reverse' or 'other side' of psychoanalysis, which was delivered in 1969–1970. There are various second-hand accounts (e.g. Bracher, 1993; Fink, 1995). Some Belgian Lacanians have been devoted to an exploration of the four discourses, and they have published in English (e.g. Quackelbeen, 1997; Verhaeghe, 1995).

Lacan speaks in the seminar of a *'discourse without speech'* (Lacan, 2007: 12) and this gives us an opening to think of relations that are instantiated as much in institutional practices as in ways of speaking – relations which we might even, to borrow a phrase from Foucault (1969/1972), see as 'discursive practices'. Lacan makes it clear that discourse is not something that should be reduced to speaking and writing. It is, he says, 'a necessary structure that goes well beyond speech', and it 'subsists in certain fundamental relations'. These fundamental relations are maintained by language, but they are, he argues, much larger; they go much further than effective utterances.

Psychology in the discourse of the university

The institutional break with the IPA, and so with Lagache, and the reorganization of the psychoanalytic movement in France provided Lacan with a context, a 'surface of emergence' we might say, for reading the organization of contemporary discourse as an indictment of psychology as part of the discourse of the university. Lacan's comments in *L'envers* link discourse, epistemology and the phenomenon of otherness in the constitution of subjects and objects in thought-provoking ways. However, the precise way in which psychology functions in this discourse requires further elaboration. Let us turn to a more detailed account of the role of psychology within the discourse of the university, and this account will also serve to introduce and illuminate the positions and terms Lacan employs.

The terms Lacan uses, which are rooted in accounts of clinical practice and a particular reading of Freud, take on certain specific functions in each of the four discourses. It will be necessary, then, to describe some of the general characteristics of the terms as they function as Lacanian concepts as well as the aspect that they take on by virtue of their relation to the other terms in their special position in the discourse of the university. The 'discourse of the university' is one of the sets of 'fundamental' 'stable relations' within which 'effective utterances' are inscribed. What I want to do here is to elaborate Lacan's argument about the discourse of the university with specific reference to psychology. This means that the distinctive character of psychology as an academic discipline will then give a further particular meaning to each term.

Psychological knowledge functions as agent in relation to the Other

The first thing to note about psychology is the way it functions through the accumulation of a corpus of knowledge about human behaviour and thinking which is presented as potentially, if not actually, universal. On the one side, at the level of micro-social processes, psychology's devotion to detailed 'sampling' of populations is designed to give a representative character to its findings. Notwithstanding the oft-repeated adherence to testing only for the 'null hypothesis' in laboratory-experimental designs (that is, the hypothesis that there is no significant difference between the experimental group and the control group), psychological reports in journals and textbooks then do typically represent the discipline as marked by scientific 'discovery'.

On the other side, on the broader macro-social scale, psychology's attention to 'cross-cultural' issues again marks the way in which its knowledge should be taken as one that will eventually be universalizable. Even the most cautious traditions in 'cultural psychology', which eschew generalizations about human behaviour across cultures, do still posit universal qualities of human psychology that would account for this very variability. It is thus the corpus of *knowledge* in psychology that operates as the driving force in the discipline, and it is this knowledge that addresses each student of psychology or subject of psychological research. Thick US psychology textbooks are testaments to the weight of this dead but effective knowledge on the minds of the living student in contemporary psychology departments. In Lacanian terms, such generalized or generalizable knowledge is a set of signifiers that defines the nature and limits of a discursive field. Signifiers are the sound images that carry concepts around in a language, the material elements that are chained together in a field of knowledge. This field of knowledge, the 'battery of signifiers' confronts each individual subject. That is, the field of signifiers – in journals, textbooks, exam papers, degree certificates and registers of chartered psychologists – is something that cannot be mastered by any one subject. In Lacan's representation of the discourse of the university this knowledge is written as 'S_2', that is, it is a series of signifiers that go beyond specific dominant signifiers that anchor a field of knowledge. I shall say more about those dominant signifiers in a moment. We might say that the set of signifiers consists of a set of statements defined by regularities that ensure and enforce agreement and adherence. They may thus operate as part of an institutional apparatus, and this is indeed what they do in the case of psychology.

Psychological knowledge provides researchers with the ability to define psychological issues as being of a certain kind and the methodological paradigms that determine the way issues should be investigated. However, this ability is only available within certain strict parameters, and it is the knowledge itself that stands in the position of the *agent*. A subject cannot master this field of signifiers, but uses it and is used by it in the process. To speak about psychology to others as an expert from within an academic institution or clinic is to assume a speaking position in *relation* to certain kinds of audience. The audience for psychological statements is also then positioned by virtue of this kind of address as the *Other* of the agent. We might usefully think of this audience as constituted, in discursive terms, in a particular kind of 'subject position' upon which certain sets of attributes are endowed and assumed. To speak in the position of agent from within the corpus of psychological knowledge, then, is to set oneself in a certain kind of relation to others.

We can represent this psychological 'knowledge' as in a relation to a certain kind of other insofar as it manifests the discourse of the university thus:

$$S_2 \text{ (psychological knowledge)} \quad \rightarrow \quad a \text{ (addressee of the psychologist)}$$

In this way psychological knowledge functions as agent in relation to the Other. The nature of this 'other' in relation to psychological knowledge will be defined in more detail presently.

A master signifier operates as the truth of psychological knowledge

Psychological knowledge requires a guarantee that it is correct, a *master signifier* that will function in such a way that those new to the discipline – students, the lay public, journalists seeking information about new discoveries to relay to their readers, researchers from other academic disciplines including psychoanalytic studies – will see that it rests upon something. A master signifier, which Lacan writes as S$_1$, holds things in place in the position of truth. Here we need to distinguish between the most powerful court of appeal summoned within the discipline to deal with dissenters, which is that of empirical investigation in Anglo-American positivist psychology, and the more immediate unreflexive appeal that is made to founding fathers or discoverers when psychology is taught to others (either taught in the sense of direct classroom or lecture teaching or in the didactic modes of address typically adopted by researchers in the face of 'non-psychologists'). A *master signifier* in this case would be invoked when it is said that 'Skinner demonstrated that' (a certain pattern of behaviour exists in the presence of a certain contingency of reinforcement) or 'Chomsky established that' (a satisfactory account of human language development must rest on a conception of semantic structures which cannot be simply learnt). It would, of course, be as problematic to summon 'Freud' or 'Lacan' as master signifiers to warrant an argument. In addition to these proper names there are other terms in the discipline of psychology that anchor the field of knowledge in this way, signifiers such as 'reliability' and 'validity'.

The cumulative character of psychological knowledge is thus underpinned by past masters who, when invoked, function to guarantee the *truth* of psychological statements. They operate as the *truth* of psychological knowledge not in terms of empirical veracity but in a sense closer to institutional requirements that, to speak in Foucauldian terms for a moment, a certain 'regime of truth' must be assumed for the knowledge to work. This kind of analysis draws attention to the way the democratic pretensions of psychology belie the necessary link with masters. These master signifiers are often the names of psychologists in the tradition who can be trusted to have laid the foundations for theoretical and methodological systems in the discipline and who signify that what psychology discovers is the truth. These psychologists are not directly present to us in a lecture theatre to wield authority, but their names operate as master signifiers. We can represent this aspect of the relationship between these terms thus:

$$\frac{S_2 \text{ (psychological knowledge)}}{S_1 \text{ (master signifiers as guarantee)}}$$

Here, a master signifier operates as the truth of psychological knowledge. In this part of the representation of the discourse of the university the 'truth' of psychology lies, as it were, 'underneath' psychological knowledge, but the nature of this metaphorical position underneath requires further attention.

The function of the bar between psychological knowledge and the master signifier

The line that divides psychological knowledge as agent from the master signifiers which function as its truth is the '*bar*' in Lacanian theory that is used to designate a relationship of 'repression'. But as we are concerned with symbolic functions in social relationships here rather than the psychic operations in a single individual the nature of this 'repression' needs to be elaborated more specifically in relation to this domain and insofar as it pertains to this relation between terms in certain positions. If we take the account given so far of the way in which the names of eminent psychologists function as 'master signifiers' to guarantee the truth of psychological knowledge, for example, we may expect that psychologists would respond with a series of objections to this. They might claim that these figures are respected but repeatedly challenged and that it is the nature of psychological inquiry that no theoretical framework is taken for granted in the discipline. But it is here that the 'repressed' relationship to the founding fathers becomes clearer in the discursive arrangements of psychological knowledge, for the appeal to these figures precisely functions *despite* this explicit disavowal of filiations with them. What studies in discursive and rhetorical psychology have been so good at is in demonstrating how appeals to things outside language or specific markers of national identity are summoned to anchor reality claims even at the same time as speakers make a pretence to be, and perhaps believe themselves to be, undecided. The studies of race and racism are key examples of this work (Wetherell and Potter, 1992). Language in the service of ideology and power requires rhetorical concealment of what it summons and assumes as the 'truth' of its statements. This concealment is the function of the bar between psychological knowledge and the master signifier.

Another aspect of the role of specific names or terms as master signifiers will be returned to in later sections of this chapter. But first, we need to turn again to the 'other' of psychological knowledge, and how it is constituted by those researchers who seek to claim authority and adopt the position of agent.

The psychological subject is the lost object

One of the ways that psychology as a discipline repeatedly wards off reflexive awareness about itself as a form of knowledge, which is about the very people who produce it, is to enforce a divide between psychological researchers and 'subjects' of research. Even when the term 'subject' is prohibited, as it has been by the British Psychological Society, because the term is seen as demeaning of the humanity of those who participate in psychological studies, the research is still conducted, within the dominant laboratory-experimental paradigm in the discipline, as being about *others*. In academic institutions, particularly in the United States, psychology students must serve time as subjects in studies, and these subjects are representative of the peculiar subject position that is constituted by researchers.

The 'other' of psychological knowledge is thus an object whose behaviour and internal mental qualities must be studied intensively, but the paradoxical nature of this object is such that the subject must both exemplify all that there is in human psychology, they must be the perfect rounded psychological being, and at the same time they must be sufficiently other to the researcher and unable to have awareness about what they are doing – that is, they must be lacking that which is to be discovered in the course of the research. The addressee of psychological knowledge, the subject to which the psychologist directs their findings and about which, we are invited to assume, psychological knowledge alone can provide a correct understanding, is thus in a position of both awe and contempt. This other is both necessary and lacking, and the task of the psychological researcher is, at the same time, to impress and dismiss this object.

In Lacanian terms, and here in the discourse of the university, this object is referred to as the '*objet petit a*', the always elusive cause of activity. This little object, which is other to the agent in the discourse of the university, cannot be captured and studied in itself. When we are in love with someone, something causes our attraction that cannot in itself be specified. If you could specify what exactly you loved about someone the effect of love would disappear, and the *objet petit a* always threatens to disappear. It is object cause of activity and anxiety. What the subject as *objet petit a* causes for the experimenter as a simple collection of behaviours or decision-making processes cannot be completely captured or represented, and this is where talk of 'confounding variables', 'demand characteristics' and 'volunteer traits' floods in to fill the gaps. The subject stands in the position of the ideal psychological subject represented in psychology journals and textbooks, but that ideal subject is 'lost' by the time we reach the laboratory to observe it. The *objet petit a*, this is also always already a lost object. One can also see the way the subject in a psychological experiment functions as object cause of anxiety when it seems possible that they will behave badly and fail to confirm the hypothesis of the experimenter. They cause the experimenter anxiety. So, the relationship depicted above can be reformulated as follows:

$$S_2 \text{ (psychological knowledge)} \quad \rightarrow \quad a \text{ ('subject' as } objet\ petit\ a)$$

In the overarching discourse that governs the discipline, then, the psychological subject is the lost object in the position of the Other. This object is addressed by psychological knowledge that is in the position of the agent. It is worked away at, and something must appear as the product. What appears expresses something of the predicament of those who encounter psychology.

The barred subject is the product of psychological work on the object

This relationship has an effect on those who are addressed as other. That is, discursive positions function to produce forms of subjectivity. What psychology does in the discourse of the university is to produce subjects who do not really learn about themselves, as they might have hoped when they first started studying. The best they can usually hope for is to adopt a position within psychological knowledge whereby they can become 'agents' and treat *others* as the impossible elusive lost object of psychological research. Usually, though, the end result for students and subjects in the discipline of psychology is to realize that they know nothing. Practices of psychological research thus function to drive home the lesson that the knowledge that is gained by the researcher is in inverse proportion to the insight gained by the subject. The effect of the relationship between the agent and other in the discourse of the university is the production of the *barred subject*.

In Lacanian terms, the barred subject (which is written as '$\$$') is the diametric opposite of the full-blown self-present humanist subject. Lacan treats this image of the full-blown subject as a mirage that is as much a product of psychologizing practices as the kind of subjectivity provoked by laboratory-experimental psychology. Students of psychology and subjects of psychological research are treated in such a way that they become disqualified from knowing about themselves, become 'embarrassed' about the knowledge they may already have about their own psychology, and if they are to stay within the orbit of psychological knowledge they can only do so experientially as 'barred subjects'.

We can thus represent this experiential effect by summarizing the argument so far and depicting that which lies underneath the bar, below the *objet petit a*:

$$S_2 \text{ (psychological knowledge)} \quad \rightarrow \quad a \text{ ('subject' as } objet\ petit\ a)$$
$$\overline{\qquad\qquad\qquad\qquad} \qquad\qquad \overline{\qquad\qquad\qquad\qquad}$$
$$S_1 \text{ (master signifiers as guarantee)} \quad \$ \text{ (product of psychology)}$$

The function of the bar between the psychological subject as object and barred subject

The relationship between psychology's object (as a subject which stands in the position of *objet petit a*) and the barred subject which is the result of psychological practice (including laboratory experimentation and other modes of address to 'non-psychologists' adopted by those who speak from the position of agent within psychological knowledge) is, again, one of 'repression', and represented here again by the bar.

Mainstream psychological research is periodically condemned as being 'dehumanizing' by those in the discipline who look to a 'new paradigm' which might go about its work in way that is more respectful of human beings (e.g. Reason and Rowan, 1981). This often also provokes a flight into humanistic psychology and its promise of a form of subjectivity that is fully present to itself and integrated (Parker, 1999b). That is, the fantasy operating in humanistic psychology precisely illustrates the way in which the production of the barred subject operates through a process of repression. To believe that one is a subject who masters the field of signifiers and is perfectly transparent to oneself as one uses language is as grandiose and self-defeating in humanist discourse as it is when psychological experts in positivist discourse express it. While this humanistic response does capture something of the surface processes by which psychologists treat people, it responds in such a way that fails to escape the logic of this discourse. This is why we argue that the barred subject is the product of psychological work on the object.

Impossibility and inability

What humanist responses to the dehumanizing activities that the discipline of psychology has engaged in for over a century now miss is that the psy-complex has already left open some spaces, positions in its discourse for the humanist subject to step into. But the positions are traps. What Lacan's account of the discourse of the university helps us to see in the rhetoric and practice of psychology is the way that no position is self-sufficient. Not only is each specific term in the positions set out by the discourse of the university untenable but also the *relations* between the terms are marked by impossibility and inability. We have looked at the 'bar' that separates the agent from truth and the one that separates the Other and the product, but the relations between agent and other and between the product and truth in this discourse are no less problematic.

The transmission of knowledge between agent and other is marked by 'impossibility'. Psychologists want others to take them seriously. They want to make a link between their knowledge and those to whom they speak, but they are continually frustrated in this. The problem is that in order to make an Other understand what a psychologist is talking about the Other either has to assume the position of *objet petit a*, in which case they are already lacking and unable to speak with authority, or to assume the position of agent, in which case they are speaking in the service of a knowledge which outstrips them. The very separation of the two positions is marked by the assumption in psychology that one should not study oneself or speak with authority about oneself. It is in this sense that the transmission of knowledge between agent and other is marked by 'impossibility'.

The relationship between the product and truth is marked by 'inability'

If there is no transmission of knowledge on the top line from agent to other, there is certainly no feedback loop running back from the barred subject as product of this discourse and the master signifiers that stand in the position of truth under the agent speaking for psychological knowledge. One way the separation is maintained is through the temporal gap between study, results and application in psychology. Psychologists working as members of the British Psychological Society, for example, know that they must not make any claims that their studies will directly and immediately benefit their objects of inquiry. Despite the hope that subjects will not leave a study with a lower level of self-esteem than they entered it with, the implicit assumption is indeed that they will lose something. They lose now, but they hope for something in the future. The promise that this will be the 'age of the brain' or that we are just one step away from decoding the gene for schizophrenia functions in this kind of way. It is in this sense that the relationship between the product and truth is marked by 'inability'.

Again, the upshot of this analysis is that the humanist alternative to positivist psychology is not really much of an alternative at all. To adopt the position of 'barred subject' as the product and loss of the discourse is not an option that humanists are likely to relish, but the other three positions are not much more palatable. The position of agent, which all self-respecting humanists would like to adopt, is a position taken by psychological knowledge to which the subject is subordinate. The position of other as subject who is studied and respected, which humanists would like to be, is a position which must be an object of suspicion which is lacking and lost. The truth that drives the discourse is something humanists would like to reach, but this would only be here to incarnate oneself as one of the master signifiers used to warrant psychological knowledge.

The discourse of the university and its reverse

This, then, is the structure of the discourse of the university. Lacan's account helps us to explore implications for epistemology in psychology of the role of discourse in the production of distance from the real and from experience at the very same moment that it fabricates our image of what lies outside representation. At stake here is the account critical psychologists may or may not want to give of the object of psychology and the organization of the psy-complex in its reproduction and transformation.

Lacan was so intensely critical of the discourse of the university because it reflected and constituted a context of bureaucratic power. Whether it was the bureaucracy of the Soviet Union that used Marxist vocabulary to mystify the masters as well as the slaves, or the apparatus of the IPA that used a psychoanalytic vocabulary to form patients and trainees in the image of their analysts, Lacan was equally scathing. To speak of the 'university' in this way does, as I indicated earlier, reflect something of the frustration that Lacan experienced at the hands of those who wanted to render psychoanalysis into something acceptable to bourgeois culture. Lacanians since have been suspicious of the university as an institution, for it is the kind of disciplinary apparatus that strips ideas of their radical potential. The university will speak of sexuality but in the best possible taste and it will study revolutions as long as it does not have to reflexively position itself in a revolutionary process. 'Paradigm revolutions' in psychology have actually, as you may know, been the most genteel of affairs.

There are implications here for epistemology in psychology, and how we might want to develop psychoanalytic alternatives within and against the discipline of psychology, but also for 'critical psychologists' who want to understand better the function of psychoanalysis on the broader terrain of the psy-complex. Psychoanalysis, with psychiatry, for example, operates within the theoretical architecture of the psy-complex much of the time as an equally efficient monitor and judge of the normal and the abnormal. However, Lacan's seminar, *L'envers*, was on the reverse of psychoanalysis, among other things a study of the context in which psychoanalysis developed and of the forces that have turned it inside out. This account of psychology in Lacan's description of the discourse of the university should now lead into a consideration of the place of 'critical psychology' and psychoanalysis as forms of knowledge complicit with and resistant to this discourse. What position within the discourses may a critical psychologist adopt? What are the implications for the way a critical psychologist might want to use psychoanalytic theory? Where do we go now to turn this account into something that might be the reverse of psychology?

In Lacan's account the discourse of the master appears to precede and lie as a kind of shadow over the other discourses, shaping them and laying out the set of positions in which the terms move around, counter-clockwise, to form the discourse of the university and then the discourse of the analyst and the discourse of the hysteric. The operation of the terms in the positions set out in this chapter, then, should not be read as a fixed grid but as a system of relationships which are overdetermined by other relationships in which we may function as agents; as master signifier, the object cause of desire or as hysteric demanding answers from others. And perhaps as other things, per- haps in discursive arrangements yet to be made and within which we may actually learn something about the nature of human psychology instead of obscuring it and ourselves at the same time.

3 Everyday behaviour(ism) and therapeutic discourse

Deconstructing the ego as verbal nucleus in Skinner and Lacan

This chapter compares arguments made by Lacan and the radical behaviourist B.F. Skinner. This unusual task is one way of tackling an argument that is sometimes made against Lacan by his critics, that he is a kind of behaviourist 'anti-humanist'.

You will see in the chapter that in order to make this comparison, and to bring out some of the crucial non-behaviourist elements of Lacan's work, I draw on three theoretical resources that have become important in 'critical psychology' in recent years. The first is 'discourse analysis', in which there is a focus on variation in speech, the way it is constructed from available resources and the functions it serves. Discourse here is understood as language organized to produce a sense of the world and of experience for speakers and listeners, writers and readers. The second resource is a combined effort by different writers sometimes brought together under the rubric 'post-structuralism', and I include here work on the historical production of discourses as systems of statements that constitute objects and the subjects who speak provided by Michel Foucault, and work on the deconstruction of systems of discourse provided by Jacques Derrida. The third resource is the rereading of psychoanalysis such that the phenomenon of subjectivity and its other, the repressed, is understood as inscribed in language rather than rooted in biology, which is where Lacan comes in.

Here you can see how important Lacan's argument is that beyond the realms of behaviour and the self lies *language*, and this is why I take discourse to be the appropriate focus for an understanding of how the phenomena psychoanalysis describes become true, embedded in the experiential field of the person and embedded in that which is experienced as outside, the underside of discourse, that which is, we say, 'unconscious'.

The relationship between behaviour and subjectivity is a fraught one in psychology, and how one understands that relationship has wide-ranging implications for how a therapist should work with clients. The theoretical debates in the discipline between behaviourism and phenomenology have been protracted but ultimately fruitless (Wann, 1964). In large part this has been because behaviourists can always re-describe the experiences phenomenologists value in terms of contingencies of reinforcement, while conversely the claims of phenomenology can always make a powerful appeal to deeply rooted common-sense humanism. The theoretical debates are refracted through therapeutic practice in disputes between behavioural therapists inspired by Skinner's work and humanists following the work of Rogers. The difference between the two positions, where behaviourists deliberately disregard the self and humanists insist that the self should be valued, is, once again, not amenable to any resolution. It is, as it were, a dialogue of the deaf.

It is precisely, I want to argue, in dialogue, in language, that conceptions of the self make themselves known, and an attention to how those conceptions appear has a number of theoretical implications for our understanding of therapeutic discourse. I will turn to these implications later, the deconstruction of the ego as a form of verbal behaviour.

In the following sections of the chapter I will be shifting from accounts of behaviour change to descriptions of the unconscious, by contrasting notions of behaviour, determinism, social context, cognition and consciousness in the writings of Skinner and Lacan. I will summarize behaviourist and psychoanalytic notions of subjectivity in order to demonstrate the ways in which the very notion of self so rigorously excluded from radical behaviourist texts emerges as a necessary condition for them to work, but also to demonstrate that this self is not the humanists' fantasy 'centre' of experience but something split twixt discourse and the outside of the text. It is a self captured and interrogated more effectively in Lacanian discourse. (The connotations that spring from that last sentence express my own ambivalence towards psychoanalysis.) I have four aims: (a) to describe the way radical behaviourist discourse accounts for the self as only a product of *verbal behaviour*; (b) to explore Lacanian psychoanalytic discourse as an alternative account that systematically reflects on the production of the self as *verbal nucleus*;

(c) to disrupt, in deconstructive spirit, the exclusion of the self in radical behaviourist discourse; and (d) to insert, as an intrinsically deconstructive third term, the Lacanian concept of the subject. Psychological theory filters out into the ordinary world, and so there are moral consequences to these debates. The therapeutic context is not an enclosed space, but one site for the elaboration of psychological discourses (Parker, 2011b). Therapy is the occasion for the development of the concept of the self (of the ego, and the correlative other of the ego, the id), but the everyday is the scene where its lasting effects are played out. I will not be reconstructing a concept of the self in its therapeutic context (or in its manifestations in therapeutic practice), but deconstructing it in a therapeutic frame (in the theoretical systems that inform therapeutic talk).

Skinner's radical behaviourism and Lacan's radical psychoanalysis

It is necessary to interpret Skinner's position, for he contradicts himself, and we could never know precisely what he intended. It may be more accurate to say that the characterization of Skinnerianism that follows is that of the radical behaviourist discourse in its broadest forms, forms that include the accounts of radical behaviourists who themselves attempt to interpret Skinner for their own purposes. Similarly, I treat the Lacanian position as a discourse for which (both as a conceptual necessity and as a notorious characteristic of Lacan's own writing) it is impossible to reconstruct one author's position.

Behaviour

A key point that distinguishes Skinnerian instrumental conditioning from Pavlovian classical conditioning is the notion of the operant. Operant behaviour is not *evoked*, hooked out of the organism, but emitted. It is sent out to meet what it may and discover the possibilities that the contingencies of reinforcement have provided (Skinner, 1950). It is this notion of the operant that allows Skinner (1977) to distance himself from what he terms the *primitive behaviourism* of Watson (1913). This account of the operant also permits the following charitable gloss of the radical behaviourist position:

> A rat is in some sense free to press a lever when it is placed in a Skinner box. . . . Much unnecessary misunderstanding might have been avoided if operant behavior had by convention been termed 'acts' or 'bits,' and if discriminative stimuli had been termed 'cues', 'signals,' or even 'antecedents' or 'circumstances.'
>
> (Blackman, 1980: 101)

The operant can be taken here, in an account that already bends towards humanist discourse (and that employs the rhetorical trick of anthropomorphizing the rat to do so), to be a function of the specifically *human* constitution and behaviour that the patterns of language, of reinforcement work upon. *Needs*, such as hunger and thirst, could be expressed simply as a function of the rate of response, but here the suggestion is that it is action given meaning by reinforcement. Behaviour is continuous in a properly radical behaviourist account. It could never, as methodological behaviourists attempt to have it, be broken out of the flow of experience (enough to be measured). It is always welded to context.

Something peculiar happens when we turn to language. Skinner's (1957) work on verbal behaviour will be discussed below, but first I want to turn to the Lacanian view of desire in language, for this extends the Skinnerian account of the operant as part of the flow of action. Human language differs from that of animal communication insofar as meaning outstrips the immediate function of the message, or the attempt to simply denote something. Animal communication is distinguished 'by the fixed correlation of its signs to the reality that they signify' (Lacan, 1977: 84). There is, in discourse, a continuous 'surplus' of connotation. Discourse is organized within the symbolic order, and in this order the processes of metaphor and metonymy provide a setting for verbal 'behaviour' that is in flux, continually shifting meanings anchored only in the enduring structures of the family, patriarchy, the law of the father, and, ultimately, the meaning invested, in this culture, in the phallus.

Lacan, discussing Freud's (1920) discussion of the *fort/da* game (in which the German terms *fort* [gone] and *da* [there] come to stand, in a game played by Freud's grandson, for the absence and presence of his mother), makes the connection between human activity and language: 'the moment in which desire becomes human is also that in which the child is born into language' (Lacan, 1977: 103). Just as the terms in language substitute for the image of the mother, so the operation of metonymy describes the continual displacement of one term by another through the person's life and the impossibility of returning to the original relation with her: 'desire is a metonymy' (Lacan, 1977: 175). Such continual movement in language (where, in Lacan's use of Saussurean linguistics, signifiers fall to the level of signifieds and then slide under the realm of signifiers), does not mean that action or speech is the result of random events or free will. Lacan, and Skinner, leave nothing to chance.

Determinism

Skinner is a determinist, and it is his determination to locate the controlling variables of behaviour in the environment that has let him in for attack from those concerned to emphasize the role of agency: 'The variables of which human behavior is a function lie in the environment' (Skinner, 1977: 1). As well as taking into account the way the environment functions in the evolution of species, Skinner discusses the role of the environment in producing the repertoire of behaviour that 'converts each member of the species into a person' (ibid.). Language is the key: 'self-knowledge, consciousness, or awareness became possible only when the species acquired verbal behavior, and that was very late in its history' (Skinner, 1977: 10). One of the consequences of this claim is that although conceptions of self and agency are errors, this need not lead to the position that they *must* be dispelled to pave the way for a return to a more natural way of being.

It is possible to read Skinner as supporting a radical behaviourist position (in which a theoretical account is provided of the emergence of consciousness in language) *against* methodological behaviourism (in which the account is part of a technology of prediction and control) (Day, 1983). At one point Skinner is careful to insist only that the origin for behaviour should not be located in the individual: 'The mistake . . . *is* to put the responsibility anywhere, to suppose that somewhere a causal sequence is initiated' (Skinner, 1973: 78). This does not mean that the person's activity within the stream of social interaction is denied, and it has been argued that although Skinner does assume total determinism, operant reinforcement theory does not require that assumption (Vorsteg, 1974). We could take this line of argument to be useful in attacking the mechanistic conceptions of determinism that warrant experimental work (always) on others. The experience of meaning as always determined (reflecting and pointing to something else) is a necessary starting point for systematic reflection on oneself.

Just as Skinner is a strict determinist, so Lacan insists that there is nothing random about the operations of the symbolic. It has always been a central tenet of psychoanalytic theory that psychic determinism operates in the production of *parapraxes* (slips, mishandled or bungled actions): '*In my experience I have observed nothing arbitrary in this field, for it is cross-checked in such a way that it escapes chance*' (Lacan, 1964/1973: 45; emphasis in original). The *psychic* nature of this determination of meaning is shifted, along with a shift of attention to the unconscious, away from the behaviour of the individual to the structure of language and the myths of the verbal community:

> Symbols in fact envelop the life of man [*sic*] in a network so total . . .
> that they give the words that will make him faithful or renegade, the law
> of the acts that will follow him right to the very place where he is not
> yet and even beyond his death.
>
> (Lacan, 1977: 68)

Lacan's insistence on the impossibility of chance, and his adherence to an orthodox Freudian account of psychic determinism, separates him from the more individualist and humanist psychoanalysts who have found favour with Anglo-American academic psychology (Erikson, Fromm, Bettelheim). The development of Freud's ideas in America has, claims Lacan, involved the adaptation of psychoanalytic theory to a competitive culture. Alongside the attempts to cure individuals by adapting them to their circumstances (rather than helping them to question those circumstances) there have been attempts to found a more adaptable psychoanalysis on an account of the rational ego. With Freud's (1933) dictum 'Where Id was, there Ego shall be' in mind, ego-psychology reconstructs the ego as the component of the personality that is responsible for directing behaviour. It is the inner monitor, and a special type of agency that can, it is imagined, stand outside determination. Lacan has been concerned to demonstrate that this ego is 'formed of a verbal nucleus . . . dependent on the signifier' (Lacan, 1977: 89).

MacCorquodale (1969), commenting on the relation between the Skinnerian notion of the operant and verbal behaviour, points out that if it were possible to know what operants a person had, it would then be possible to predict precisely what the person was going to say. The reason why it is not possible to predict speech is that radical behaviourist discourse draws a strict distinction between the operant and the response:

> A response is what repeats and can be counted. However, the recycling aspect of bar pressing and key pecking is an intentional artifact of the experimental situation which does not occur in verbal behavior, whose formal properties tell us nothing about where the boundaries of its component responses are located.
>
> (MacCorquodale, 1969: 835)

In similar fashion, the continual cross-checking in psychoanalysis over the speech of the analysand focuses on the determination of repetitions, signs of the repressed. Current speech will provide new material for an understanding of this network, but that speech is also determined by the structure of desire. There is a tension between what is already set into the history of the person (and into the context of his or her action) and what keeps pushing into that history. Accounts of ideology that draw upon psychoanalysis have been concerned with the simultaneous desire for coherence of self and impossibility of that coherence: 'the human subject is de-centred, constituted by a structure that has no "centre" either, except in the imaginary misrecognition of the "ego", i.e. in the ideological formations in which it recognizes itself' (Althusser, 1971: 201).

Social context

Operant behaviour is welded to context, so much so that it would be possible to see verbal forms as being, in ethnomethodological terms, indexical (Filmer, 1972). For human beings, operant behaviour is intrinsically social, and this is not only because the reinforcement depends, in most cases, on the activity of another person. Reinforcement is organized within culture: "'The Languages" studied by the linguist are the reinforcing practices of verbal communities' (Skinner, 1957: 461). The insistence on the immersion of the organism in the linguistic practices that comprise the verbal community is manifested in different ways by radical behaviourists on hard and soft ends of the research spectrum (represented respectively in the pages of the *Journal of the Experimental Analysis of Behavior* and in the journal *Behaviorism*).

On the hard end are those who do link radical behaviourist theory with methodological behaviourist practice. Here the operant is always directed *to* something, for it cannot exist in a free-floating state. This idea is captured in the claim that it is possible (and necessary) to give an operational definition in which the description of behaviour is always meshed into the net of behavioural contingencies: 'the important properties of the operant relation are empirical and not logical' (Catania, 1973: 110). Here the shift of emphasis to the social, a shift that would be consonant with the shift discourse analysis facilitates away from the supposed intentions of an author for a text, is marked at the cost of dissolving *any* conception of agency (in order that the identification of contingencies should be possible). On the softer end of the spectrum are statements of the variety 'the rat is free', in which the argument is that 'reinforcement does not cause the organism to do anything . . . it equips . . . it enables' (Day, 1977: 226). (The author of this statement, Willard Day, is then able to combine a radical behaviourist academic practice with devout Christian faith.) What is important here is that the difference between these two ends of the spectrum is about what it is possible for a scientist to capture empirically, not how far the verbal community captures and conditions the human subject.

In Lacan's work, because the individual self is displaced from centre stage in favour of the *relations* between self and others, in relations organized by language, behaviour cannot but be social. Once the organism is enveloped within language, biological needs cannot be expressed (or satiated) in an unmediated form. Speech, according to Lacan (1977), within language structured by the symbolic order, is also conditioned by an intersubjectivity in which there is meaning only for the subject who is speaking, insofar as speech calls upon the response of another subject: 'there is no speech without a reply, even if it is met only with silence' (Lacan, 1977: 40), and 'the function of language is not to inform but to evoke' (p. 86). In speaking to a person, 'I intimate to him the subjective function that he will take on again in order to reply to me, even if it is to repudiate this function' (Lacan, 1977: 87). This statement does evoke as always already aggressive the relation set up between persons. What Lacan calls the 'struggle for prestige' (p. 69), however, is dependent on others: 'the desire for recognition dominates in these determinations the desire that is to be recognized, by preserving it as such until it is recognized' (p. 69).

The phenomenological influences on Lacan include Hegel (1807/1977), more accurately Alexandre Kojève's (1969) account of Hegel, whose lectures Lacan, and other influential French writers such as Sartre, attended (Descombes, 1980). From Kojève's Hegel comes the notion of a dialectic of recognition between self and others in the formation of self-consciousness. The dialectic, which sets up positions of Master (who is able to gain the recognition from another) and Slave (who gives that recognition at the cost of being treated as object), is driven by desire which cannot be established without an Other: 'desire is the desire of the Other' (Lacan, 1964/1973: 38). What is important here is the way phenomenology is used to elaborate an account of intersubjective *violence*. (The notion of a desire for recognition appears in liberal humanist watered-down form in Rogers' (1961) work.) Lacan does make use of other forms of psychoanalysis, including that of Klein, to emphasize that 'aggressive motives . . . lie hidden in all so-called philanthropic activity' (Lacan,1977: 13), a conclusion being that 'we place no trust in altruistic feeling' (p. 7). However, the misanthropy expressed here is not so much rooted in the drives as in the intersubjective relationship of the master/slave dialectic by which Hegel 'provided the ultimate theory of the proper function of aggressivity in human ontology' (p. 26).

Cognition

Just as Skinner (1977) contrasts his position with that of primitive behaviourism, so he also rejects the trend, increasingly gaining strength in psychology, of cognitive behaviourism. He argues that when the Greeks 'invented the mind', they also manufactured the assumption that there were, in the mind, 'internal copies . . . cognitive surrogates of the real world' (Skinner, 1977: 5). Skinner was against the view peddled by cognitive 'science' that we should locate the objects of explanation inside the heads of people to understand what they are doing: 'The body responds to the world, at the point of contact, making copies would be a waste of time' (Skinner, 1977: 139). An expression of this view also appears in more scientistic guise earlier: 'We operate in one world – the world of physics' (Skinner, 1953: 139).

In verbal behaviour, the notion of direct *contact* with the world is expressed in Skinner's term *tact.* The notion of tact, and of a real world of some sort, is necessary to Skinner's empiricist worldview, but it can also, when it is thought of in relation to the many verbal communities we encounter, undermine the fantasy of measurement. Once the variety of responses to the world is taken seriously, the world of physics becomes useless as a touchstone for description, and we are forced closer to a phenomenological view that inspires the following claims (made in the context of a sympathetic comparison of Skinner and Sartre) by Kvale and Greness (1975):

> There are a multitude of different behavioral relationships to the world and it is meaningless to choose one as the correct objective approach to the real world . . . by discarding the prejudice of the physical world, the 'outer' world becomes our meaningful, lived world.
>
> (Kvale and Greness, 1975: 44–45)

The phenomenological account that first softens and then progressively undermines Skinner's position brings us, once again, to Lacan's account. The way it is used in Lacan's version of post-Freudian theory, however, is to oppose the objectification of the ego as the site of rational thought. The ego is, rather, to be thought of as reproduced in language by means of speech: 'dependent on the signifier . . . a topological phenomenon whose distribution in nature is as sporadic as the dispositions of pure exteriority that condition it' (Lacan, 1977: 32–34). Although it is true that Lacan traces 'the essential structure of the ego' (p. 142) to the pre-linguistic (Hegelian/ Kojèvean) struggle for recognition, it is the symbolic order that supports the (mis-)recognition that results from the earliest awareness of a relationship to the (m)other in the mirror phase.

It is possible here to follow the reinterpretation of Freud's (1933) dictum 'Where Id was, there Ego shall be' as the aim of psychoanalysis to illustrate the shift of emphasis from internal mechanism to external contingencies. As it stands, the project of psychoanalysis, as expressed by Freud here, appears compatible with a form of cognitivist psychology, but Lacan argues that we should, in order to return to the true meaning of Freud, return to the original German phrase: '*Wo es war, soll ich werden.*' Instead of seeing more, and more of the id (*Es* or *It*) *as* being appropriated by the ego (*Ich* or I), Lacan argues that Freud is really saying that within the id as locus of *being*, that I (or sense of self) should be permitted to emerge (Lacan, 1977: 128). Rather than strengthening the ego as if it were an inner entity, Lacan insists that the true subject should emerge from its place in the unconscious. Lacan even indicates that he would have been happier with the translation of the German Es (*id*, more accurately *It*) as *the self* (p. 129).

If we turn to the conception of what the locus of being or the true subject of the unconscious consists of, we see that what is being described is the cumulative record of the person's experiences. It is not some inner homunculus that is being referred to, but a repertoire and its correlative repressions. It is in this sense that the unconscious is conceptualized by Lacan as a *memory* (1977: 215). Psychoanalysis, then, has the aim of enabling the person to account for his or her past, to become where he or she was produced rather than in a position in which he or she is both ignorant of his or her past and objectified in that position as the ego. An alternative translation of '*Wo es war, soll ich werden*' is 'I must come to that place where that was' (Lacan, 1977: 171).

Lacan provides a description in which subjectivity is constructed within language as a *text* (p. 146). Personal history is patterned through the text we produce and must be understood in the context of the text. It is not necessary to turn to internal mechanisms to explain what really is occurring for the subject. Because 'the subject is always a fading thing that runs under the chain of signifiers' (Lacan, 1973: 194), it is the movement of those signifiers, and what is hidden, excluded, that can be understood as the unconscious of the text.

Consciousness

For Skinner, consciousness has to be explained as the exception rather than as the rule of behaviour. Most of behaviour is reinforced without any conscious mediation. What is conscious involves the elaboration into awareness of discriminatory responses to behaviour. Linguistic self-reference, in Skinner's (1957) terms *intraverbal, echoic* or *textual*, is conditioned by the relationship between the person and others. There is also a second-level form of verbal behaviour that is both dependent on verbal behaviour and provides a commentary on it. (This is a form of talk which talks about talk, but which is just another layer rather than an expression of something 'deeper' or something 'behind' talk.) This second level is 'autoclitic'. Autoclitic behaviour gives the *effect* of controlling verbal behaviour, and our engagement with this reinforces the illusion of an inner, substantive, autonomous self (see Skinner, 1957: 315).

The initial activity of the organism before the generation of awareness and self-awareness is best termed *non-conscious.* It is not, in psychoanalytic terms, unconscious (*pace* Chandra, 1976). There are distinctive operations in the unconscious. What has been present and is now absent is different from what has never been present at all.

This point is captured in an interpretation of repression compatible with a radical behaviourist position, and here formulated to interpret Freud in Skinnerian terms, in which what is punished does not just vanish: 'the role of punishment is simply to strengthen (increase the probability of) an incompatible response. The "repressed" response *continues* in strength; its probability is not reduced' (Chandra, 1976: 59).

The unconscious does not precede the formation of the self but can only arise as a phenomenon when language has been acquired. For Lacan, the unconscious is not a dark store of irrational fantasies, nor a system of biologically based drives that determine the life of the neonate as *non-conscious*. The habitual activities and patterns of learnt behaviour existing before the development of the human species (as Skinner points out, an essentially linguistic achievement) are non-conscious. Once self-awareness has been produced, the subject has to deal with a system of language, the symbolic, which is itself experienced as Other: 'The unconscious is that part of the concrete discourse, in so far as it is transindividual, that is not at the disposal of the subject in reestablishing the continuity of his conscious discourse' (Lacan, 1977: 49).

Attending to the work of the unconscious, then, means that the slips and figurative uses of language present in the speech of the person can be taken to be signs of symptomatic gaps in the person's account of his or her past. This does not mean that something underneath speech needs to be released: 'Certainly we must be attentive to the 'un-said' that lies in the holes of the discourse, but this does not mean that we are to listen as if to someone knocking on the other side of a wall' (Lacan, 1977: 93).

One of the central tenets of the cognitivist account of psychology is identified and opposed here. The opposition to the notion of an *inner self*, a *ghost in the machine*, is a point that unites phenomenology with radical behaviourism:

> the hypothesis of a consciousness, or a homunculus, enclosed in the organism and guiding behavior as a pilot guides his airplane, must eventually be discarded from a scientific psychology . . . Behavior is no mere indicator of an inner state, man [*sic*] is his behavior to the world.
> (Kvale and Greness,1975: 42)

The patterns and consequences of that behaviour are integrated into the subject's life history in such a way, however, that memory of past events is affected by and reflected in her speech. What is always *Other* to the subject, then, as the symbolic, 'is the locus of that memory . . . called the unconscious' (Lacan, 1977: 215).

The reflections of past events lie in what is blocked out of the subject's discourse. Terms will be replaced by other terms. What has been repressed continues in strength in the subject's repertoire, but, through the operation of metaphor, it is not expressed. Thom (1976) put it like this:

The snag in the tissue marks the place where the original signifier is, as it were, vertically suspended. It has been 'displaced' and has fallen to the rank of the signified. However, although it has fallen . . . it persists as a repressed signifier itself. This persistence (and insistence) of a repressed chain is precisely what gives poetry, that most metaphorical of arts, the quality of saying what it says as much as by what is not there as by what is.

(Thom 1976: 454)

The subject's unconscious, then, insofar as it can be said to belong to the subject, is 'the level of symbolic overdetermination' (Lacan, 1977: 14). It is the confluence of affectively charged figures of speech holding a multitude of connotations which continually outstrip what was intended. These meanings are held in language shared by subjects in verbal communities (and sub-communities), and the Lacanian description of the unconscious reinforces the social character of the action that people engage in. It is this social character of action, and of the ego as a piece of the action, that provides a more radical conception of the self than that offered by radical behaviourism (which attempts to explain *away* the self). The ego, the sense of self, is felt as private, but this feeling of privacy is a function of how the public sphere, the symbolic order is organized.

The public and the private

Part of Skinner's appeal lies in his refusal to speculate about what is happening inside the person. The focus is on the public realm, the outer realm of verbal practices. Phenomenology, which explores the meanings the subject gives to the world, privileges the interior, private realm. It would appear from many of the accounts given within the psychoanalytic tradition, including those in Lacan's work, that the only counterweight to the behaviourist public, constructed, self, is an essential introspectively grounded private self. However, an exploration of Skinner's description of the nature of 'private' stimuli and the fiction of the self uncovers some important aspects of subjectivity that radical behaviourism routinely denies. Hidden within radical behaviourist discourse is a notion of the self which Skinner disavows, a notion of the self as *other* to his discourse, a notion of the self that calls for that very psychoanalytic theory that both Skinner (as opponent of the self) and humanists (celebrants of the self) repress.

Private stimuli

The learning of the language of public stimuli, and the employment of language to bring about certain effects, is dealt with by Skinner in his work on *tacts* (where a tact denotes direct unmediated contact with the world): 'both speaker and listener are represented as in contact with a common object, to which the speaker's response refers' (Skinner, 1957: 130). But what is the *common object* when the verbal community attaches verbal behaviour to a private stimulus that it has no direct contact with? Skinner suggests four ways in which the attachment may be accomplished. The first three ways rest on an assumption that the private stimulus is *already* individuated. It then has only to be connected with the appropriate forms of verbal behaviour: (a) the appropriate verbal behaviour might accompany the stimulus, where a feeling of pain, for example, can be evoked with reference to the occurrence of visible physical damage; (b) some correlative behaviour may be the occasion for verbal behaviour, and Skinner suggests that this type of collateral response is the most common process for marking a private stimulus (a pain may be indicated by grimacing, and the grimacing acts as index and intermediary); or (c) the stimulus may once have been evident to both speaker and listener, been reinforced, and may only later have become unobservable to others (a variant of the first-mentioned behaviour).

Although radical behaviourism promises a constructionist account of human experience, these explanations of private stimuli are, paradoxically, less radical than the humanist social constructionist (and resolutely anti-behaviourist) positions in psychology in which, for example, emotions have been described as produced in language rather than being pre-existing (Harré, 1986) and the nature of the person has been described as a linguistic achievement (Harré and Mühlhäusler, 1990).

The task Skinner must address, if he is to follow the logic of the radical behaviourist position, the tracks of its discourse, is how such private stimuli are delimited in the first place. One possibility is that the person engages in some kind of selection and evaluation of the private stimulus which is prelinguistic or extra-linguistic. We must discount this explanation, because it presupposes the existence of a *cognitive* process with a centre, the self, speculation over which Skinner has always tried to avoid (e.g. Skinner, 1977). If there is no pre-existing set of private events (assumed by Skinner's first three suggestions) and no pre-existing cognitive apparatus to evaluate the stimuli (which would contradict the radical behaviourist framework), what option is left?

The argument so far may appear to be one concerned with logical problems in the radical behaviourist position, but I now want to turn to the fourth suggestion Skinner makes, for it is here that the issue is not so much logical inconsistencies but *linguistic* contradiction that demands that some form of subjectivity should emerge. Skinner's fourth suggestion is as follows:

the community may not need to appeal to private stimuli at all; it may reinforce a response in connection with a private stimulus, only to have the response transferred to a private event by virtue of common properties, as in metaphorical and metonymical extension.

(Skinner, 1957: 132)

The idea that the net of linguistic differentiations and semantic values which maps the private world of the person is generated by the verbal community would be consonant with radical behaviourist notions of the control of autoclitic self-referential behaviour. With Lacan's appeal to the idea that language may work by itself is the suggestion that devices such as metaphor and metonymy could *produce* private stimuli. It should be pointed out that Skinner here still resorts to the claim that the extension of language transfers a verbal response to a private event already distinguished by its common properties, and that he must make the assumption that the tact (with direct unmediated contact) is applicable to the speaker's internal world. As has been pointed out above, this 'presupposes that a speaker *can* discriminate his own behaviour as a covert, essentially private, event' (MacCorquodale, 1969: 839).

In the same way that a private stimulus stands free of adulteration before the speaker tacts it, so the speaker, we are led to imagine, stands free of context in the role of tacting agent – and at points, the image is of a consciously aware tactition. Skinner, in other words, fixes the *source* of verbal behaviour in a single point in the speaker while insisting elsewhere that this point is *constructed* (and therefore cannot be the source). As well as being an organism that produces verbal behaviour, the speaker is 'a locus – a place in which a number of variables come together in a unique confluence to yield an equally unique achievement' (Skinner, 1957: 313). This locus, though, which is manifest in the phenomenon of self-descriptive autoclitics of the self, is substantialized as a real thing, much in the way that the ego-psychologists Lacan condemns substantialize the sporadic, transitory ego.

The absence of a centre of language

Although Skinner's (1957) *Verbal Behavior* includes discussion of literature and the nature of language as the context for the production of speech, there is no consideration of theories of language as such. Lacan's work, in contrast, does draw on a theory of language, and it is a theory of language that could just as well have formed the backdrop for radical behaviourist descriptions. Saussure argued that 'Without language, thought is a vague, uncharted nebula. There are no preexisting ideas, and nothing is distinct before the appearance of language' (Saussure, 1915/1974: 112). In this theory of language, attention is shifted from speech to the system of language (the notion of structure that was to inspire French structuralism and then what became dubbed in the English-speaking world 'post-structuralism', and which was to underlie Lacan's account of the system/structure he termed the *symbolic*): this system cannot be controlled by a self. Language is labile, without centre or source: 'a difference generally implies positive terms between which the difference is set up; but in language there are only differences *without positive terms'* (Saussure, 1915/1974: 120).

An example of where the movement of language slips out of the control of a speaker can be found in Skinner's discussion of *magical mands*. The mand is 'a verbal operant in which the response is reinforced by a characteristic consequence' (Skinner, 1957: 35). Its form, then, is designed to connote command or demand. It would be tempting, even, to characterize it as reflecting the desires of the person, being used to obtain satisfaction or produce effects. Skinner does, in fact, comment on the *dynamic properties* which make the mand 'a very expressive type of operant' (Skinner, 1957: 42). The magical mand refers to the way a speaker continually creates new mands despite the fact that they could never have been reinforced. This extended operant, furthermore, 'does not exhaust the field of verbal magic' (Skinner, 1957: 48). Skinner resorts to (magical) analogy to explain its production to problematize the role of the speaker, but does not pursue the consequences that poetic language opens up, the production of meaning that contemporary post-structuralist literary theory is concerned with (Eagleton, 1983), preferring instead the more cautious and prosaic formulation that: 'Literature is the product of a special verbal practice which brings out behavior which would otherwise remain latent in the repertoires of most speakers' (Skinner, 1957: 50).

The continual metaphorical and metonymical extensions of language and the use of analogies to construct magical verbal behaviour illustrates once again, however, that meaning produced in language outstrips the repertoires of speakers or their intentions. This point also applies to the characterization of *interpretative repertoires* offered by discourse analysts in psychology (e.g. Potter and Wetherell, 1987). To say that language determines behaviour, then, is simultaneously to say that determination is based on the *indeterminacy* of meaning in language. The flux of meaning necessitates the relocation of the speaker in the verbal community. While Skinner recognizes the latent problems here, he deals with them all too briefly, in his discussion of magical mands, by relegating them to the status of marginal phenomena. Such a marginalization is crucial to maintain the privilege of the speaker in radical behaviourism. In other words, it is not marginal at all, but the closest that one could get to a centre in this account of language. Too close.

The self

In the discussion of private stimuli I pointed out that Skinner often refers to the private stimulus as if it were already individuated, ready to be labelled with the appropriate term. In much the same way, when radical behaviourists talk about the self, it *is presupposed* as being that which engages in discriminatory behaviour. This is clearly expressed in accounts of self-deception (Day, 1977), in which the route to self-understanding and spontaneity is described as running through a rational evaluation of the contingencies of reinforcement that control behaviour. Day (1977) sets up an opposition between the verbal community, on the one hand, and the discriminative behaviour of the individual on the other. The force of the radical behaviourist argument is that there is no self or subject outside its production in autoclitic verbal behaviour, but in Day's discussion spontaneity and understanding are predicated on the existence of just such a substantive inner core of self-consciousness, self-identical, present to itself, arbiter of contingencies:

> [We] . . . are essentially at the mercy of the verbal community which determines to what extent, and in what way, we can be regarded as having knowledge of what we are doing, and of what the causes of our behavior are taken to be.
>
> (Day, 1977: 233)

Day then offers an example to illustrate how a radical behaviourist can delve into the verbal behaviour surrounding a particular interpersonal event and eventually arrive at a resolution of the problem. Verbal material, an organization of talk within a particular verbal sub-community, is described as encountering and contradicting other material. Day argues that certain aspects of this behaviour can finally be extinguished, thus avoiding the reinforcement that would result from public recirculation. Once again, however, the very phenomena Day attempts to exclude, by virtue of his account being an elaboration of a radical behaviourist position, return with a vengeance to haunt his argument. Here, they are, in addition, three of the very ingredients of orthodox psychology that radical behaviourism had promised to expunge from its understanding of human action: (a) the second level (autoclitic) of verbal behaviour that Skinner described as being an effect of commentary is taken to be autonomous of the controlling variables of the verbal community, and discriminative behaviour occupies the position, in this discourse, of the *agent* of behaviour; (b) this agentic discriminative behaviour is a peculiarly privileged variety of behaviour that then stands to the rest of behaviour as if it were an inner *cognitive* process that guarantees the integrity of the person's rational evaluative capacities; (c) this autonomous process is individualized such that the condition for the verbal material to be extinguished is the (rational) separation of the *individual* from the social in which covert behaviour could be sifted until there was a resolution.

The contradiction that Day's elaboration of radical behaviourist discourse contains is one that runs through the texts signed by Skinner, too. While MacCorquodale pointed out, in his discussion of Skinner's *Verbal Behavior*, that 'speech is the last stronghold of mentalism' (MacCorquodale, 1969: 833), in Day's (1977) account mentalism remerges in the *withholding of* speech.

Skinner suggests the term *autoclitic* to describe 'behavior which is based upon or depends upon other verbal behavior' (Skinner, 1957: 315), but this neologism contains a contradiction within itself that then explodes when it is elaborated as part of a discourse that tries to account for action that continually calls for a concept of the self. The very term *auto* carries the connotations of self-directedness, of a self-centred process. An alternative term which appears in psychoanalytic discourse *is anaclitic*. This term is important for Lacan to emphasize the directedness of the drives. The sexual drives, for example, 'which become independent only secondarily, are anaclitic, "propped upon" the vital functions which furnish them with an organic source, a direction, and an object' (Laplanche and Pontalis, 1972: 179). The anaclitic nature of speech draws attention to its dependence on language. This is not to say that the solution to a problem in the organization of language (here the organization of radical behaviourist and psychoanalytic discourses) can be solved by substituting one word for another. The task of reforming language to describe and reproduce alternative forms of subjectivity is too complex and massive for one author, one book, one academic discipline. Although psychological theory and therapeutic talk trickles into the everyday world and affects behaviour and experience there, our talk is dependent on the forces moving common-sense discourse. It was just such an awareness of this dependence on everyday talk that fuelled the crisis in psychology (Parker, 1989).

Conclusions

The crisis movements in psychology that have carried a variety of discourse analysis into our part of the academic world have had an abiding horror of the technocratic fantasies of 'scientific' psychology (Parker, 1989), and the slogan of the turn to language at the beginning of the 1970s was to 'treat people as if they were human beings' (Harré and Secord, 1972: 84). Skinner was singled out for attack: as threatening to replace freedom and dignity with a 'human termite colony' (Shotter, 1975: 136); and with the destruction of human autonomy in present society producing 'the psychopolitics of B.F. Skinner, who makes the claim for the right to rule quite explicit' (Harré, 1979: 142).

Discourse analysis, running in the tracks of structuralist and post-structuralist movements in other human sciences, problematizes the very notion of the agentic human being that the earlier crisis movements appealed to. One consequence is that discourse analysis, which refuses explanations resting within the person, can have a behaviourist feel to it. The Saussurean conception of language as a system is compatible with the descriptions of the verbal community Skinner's subjects inhabit, and it is also the source of discourse theories (which break the system into contradictory discourses or repertoires). It is, then, hardly surprising that there should be this problem of discourse analysis appearing to fall into a behaviourist trap. The solution to this paradox, I have wanted to say, is not to deny the behaviourist discourse, but to work within it tactically (*pace* Skinner, so to speak), deconstructing it.

The insistence of the self within radical behaviourist discourse is not a demonstration of its lack of rigour but a sign of its failure. It is precisely its rigorous rhetorical exclusion of the self, its attempt to push the self to the margins, that is its undoing, and its failure is the failure of the fantasy that it would ever be possible to exclude the self completely from any form of discourse. It should be said that there are formulations by Lacan's supporters that mirror some of the caricatures of Skinner presented by his critics. It is claimed, for example, that, for Lacan, 'humans are no more than homeo-static mechanisms and humanisms are but momentary and contingent cohesions of sense perceptions' (Racevskis, 1983: 37).

However, psychoanalysis, particularly in its Lacanian variants, more often takes the form of a discourse that treats the self as a problem (as radical behaviourism does), but as a problem which does organize itself as a system of fantasies and defences as a necessary part of human action. The success of psychoanalytic discourse lies in its ability to understand the split in the subject between an imaginary self in language and a desiring being as the repressed other of language. The opposition between those two components of the split has to be comprehended, with neither side of the opposition privileged. Insofar as the deconstruction of the self in the radical behaviourist discourse that I have described identifies, overturns and blocks the re-emergence of an opposition between *language-behaviour* and *the self*, Lacanian psychoanalytic discourse is that deconstruction in action.

4 Socio-critical methods of investigation

Four strategies for avoiding psychoanalysis

(With Chris Dunker)

This chapter was originally co-authored with the Brazilian psycho-analyst Christian Ingo Lenz Dunker, who helped me see how some of the critical psychological interventions in qualitative research we were making in the English-speaking world were actually profoundly influenced by Lacanian ideas. This led the two of us to assemble a case for inscribing a Lacanian conceptual framework in qualitative research. We also draw on the work of the Marxist Georges Politzer, who made his own critique of psychoanalysis which is not, we think, really incompatible with Lacan. This is where the 'dialectics' comes in.

We claim in the chapter that psychoanalysis has many times in its history been defined as an anti-psychology, and so if we aim to generate, experimentally, an 'anti-psychoanalytic' approach, perhaps we may arrive at an 'anti-anti-psychology'; in other words, at a way of encountering the nature of subjectivity in contemporary society. However, this attempt at a dialectical reversal of the terms of debate set up in qualitative research – a 'sublation' as we put it in the paper – is risky. It could be read as leading us back to something we imagine is a more authentic psychology.

Another way of framing our task in the chapter is that psychology has many times in its history been defined as a form of anti-psychoanalysis, and so if we aim to generate, experimentally, an 'anti-psychological' approach, perhaps we may arrive at an 'anti-anti-psychoanalysis'; in other words, at a way of encountering the nature of subjectivity in contemporary society. In other words, we arrive back at psychoanalysis. In fact, if we take this route, we arrive at Lacanian psychoanalysis. I am sorry if this seems a bit convoluted. As we trace our way through the argument in the following pages it will make more sense.

There are various contradictory theoretical frameworks that can be employed to enrich qualitative research. These are also important resources for us in this article, and we will be emphasizing the *strategic* uses of theory to bring about political effects in research. We outline conceptual strategies for engaging with, and transcending the historical influence of, psychoanalysis in qualitative social science research. We aim to show pathways by which the researcher might tackle psychoanalysis in a more effective way than is accomplished by the standard 'defensive' procedures used to ward off psychoanalytic ideas. In this way, through the sublation of psychoanalytic categories, we show the way towards a form of 'anti-psychoanalysis'.

Socio-critical models and methods

One, two, three

Qualitative research that aims to examine 'experience' is already confronted with questions about the role that this experience plays in ideology or in challenges to ideology. Feminist methodology provides one way of theorizing the connection between the domains of political change and how political processes are lived out 'experientially', performatively at the level of the individual (e.g. Butler, 1990). Feminist perspectives attend to qualitative aspects of phenomena of all kinds, and throw into question the attempt to reduce behaviour, function, meaning or value to universal or 'natural' patterns that can then be used as points of comparison. Feminism shows how experience is not immediately accessible, because that experience is always mediated by language, institutions, discourses, culture, class position and, of course, gender. It thus connects with qualitative research that takes *mediation* seriously.

Marxist approaches are another valuable resource, and there are many implications of adopting a Marxist standpoint in qualitative research which connect with feminist perspectives. Marxism draws attention to the function of ideology, for example, and so to the always present possibility that present-day social arrangements may be operating for certain interests and against others; dialectical conceptions of social reality draw attention to the way political-economic arrangements are always in flux, in a process of change, and so we need to account in our research for why things seem to stay the same (Bensaïd, 2002). Marxist perspectives thus draw attention to the nature of social reality not as a mere collection of 'facts' or 'objects', but as a network of contradictory *forces*. The reality of any object of research is not immediately accessible because there is always a process of addition or subtraction through which something appears to us as a recognizable object. This means that a qualitative approach needs to reconstruct the political ideological strategies that produce and sustain this process of conceptual addition and subtraction through which the world then appears to us 'as it is'.

A third relevant framework that we would like to draw upon is a composite of a variety of different theoretical perspectives that are sometimes assembled under the label 'post-structuralism' (Sarup, 1988). Although this is actually quite a misleading label, it serves to bring together analyses of surveillance and confession in the work of Michel Foucault (1975/1979, 1976/1981) and the radical deconstruction of dominant systems of meaning in the writings of Jacques Derrida (1981). We take from this assemblage of theoretical vantage points the argument that it is not sufficient to study 'disciplinary' power, but that it is equally important to analyse the processes by which individual subjects come to believe that they should talk about their innermost thoughts and feelings; this is an aspect of power that incites 'confession', including confession to a qualitative researcher. For us, this framework, such as it is, entails that we pay attention to how subjectivity is produced within its own particular 'regime of truth' (Foucault, 1980). Subjectivity must be considered as a kind of *effect* of discursive practices, not as the expression of the interior voice of free and autonomous individuals.

Qualitative investigation must then question its own position when it aims to investigate phenomena, must include itself in the process that constitutes those phenomena, otherwise it will only produce and reproduce, to borrow a phrase from Karl Kraus, the 'illness of which it purports to be a cure'.

The 'deconstruction' of meaning functions here to question claims that researchers (who too often like to think of themselves as 'experts') usually make in their attempts to provide a certain fixed account which is more accurate than that given by their participants. We attempt to link this unravelling of 'expertise' with Marxist and feminist arguments by turning our research into a 'practical deconstruction'; then it is possible to move from merely interpreting the world to *changing* it; a radical interpretation that challenges the ground-rules and assumptions that serve those with power can then also lay the basis for different ways of being in the world. Here we differentiate ourselves from qualitative research that sees its tasks as either producing a re-description of reality, objects or phenomena or as providing a reinterpretation of data in a broader context, as some cognitive perspectives in sociology, anthropology and psychology attempt to do. The decision to work on a problem from within a socio-critical perspective is at the same time a choice and a bid to change the conditions which have made this problem possible.

Psychoanalysis otherwise

This brings us to our fourth critical resource, psychoanalysis, and it is this fourth resource that we will focus upon in this chapter. Psychoanalysis, like feminism, examines the way in which social structural processes are lived out by the individual subject. For psychoanalysis, as with feminism, the 'personal' is 'political', and we will also be concerned in this chapter with the way we can develop qualitative research in such a way that the 'political' aspects of 'personal' life are taken seriously without *reducing* politics to the personal level (Burman, 1998). Psychoanalysis as a clinical practice links interpretation and change at the level of the individual very much in the same way as Marxism links interpretation and change at the level of political economy. An interpretation, as a radically new way of understanding which changes relationships between the subject and others, is also something that calls into being new forms of social reality.

So we will be concerned here with the kind of interpretations qualitative researchers might make which are not content with merely changing how people view their world; we want to provoke interpretations by researchers and participants that change the texture of the world itself (Parker, 2005). In this sense, neither feminism nor Marxism is oriented to the classic problem-solving orientation that usually provides the coordinates for quantitative research. A good outcome of a piece of research may be precisely to construct a new question, or to dissolve a false problem, to draw attention to our lack of knowledge and failure to appropriately conceptualize a phenomenon. These perspectives – feminism and Marxism – are founded on conflict as an inherent premise; they are not only theories *about* conflict and methods to deal with it, they are also forms of praxis oriented to produce some change *with* conflict, extracting the consequences of that conflict.

Psychoanalysis also has strong affinities with some of the writers who are grouped together under the heading of 'post-structuralism', and this is the case insofar as they disturb and unravel the 'self-identity' of the subject. Psychoanalysis and post-structuralism both disturb and unravel the image that social scientists like to have of researchers and participants, that they are 'rational' social actors and that their 'attitudes' and 'experiences' can be discovered and described. They – psychoanalysis and post-structuralism – also both disturb and unravel the supposed unity of the different social science disciplines, whether sociology, psychology or anthropology, and call for multiple perspectives that go beyond mere 'interdisciplinary' research. (For a detailed discussion of these four resources, see Parker, 2003.) Socio-critical qualitative research does not adhere to the image of science as an accumulating knowledge process, a bureaucratic puzzle organized by stable paradigms described by Kuhn (1962) as 'normal science'. Our research rather sustains itself more on an epistemology of perpetual crisis and attends to what is problematic about knowledge, much as is described by Kuhn during times of 'paradigm crisis' and by other authors concerned with problems of method, alienation and incommensurability during the process of scientific reasoning (e.g. Feyerabend, 1978; Habermas, 1971; Koyré, 1965).

With these preliminary comments on different theoretical resources and the place of psychoanalysis in relation to other socio-critical 'models' – feminism, Marxism, post-structuralism – as the conceptual background for our argument, we will now turn to consider why psychoanalysis in particular needs to be taken seriously. Above and beyond the various arguments that can be made for psychoanalysis by those who are enthusiastic followers of certain schools and traditions, there are two crucial reasons why psychoanalysis must be taken into account in socio-critical qualitative research.

Disavowal of indebtedness

The first reason is that disciplines that constitute the 'social sciences' are heavily indebted to psychoanalytic ideas in the way they have been historically formed as separate academic subjects, as distinctive disciplines of research, and – this is the crucial point – they *disavow* that indebtedness. This disavowal requires a double move; there is pretence that psychoanalysis is of no importance and, at the same time, there is the utilization of psychoanalytic ideas in such a way as to deny their provenance. Sociology, psychology and anthropology had very close links with psychoanalysis at the beginning of the twentieth century, links that are often erased in contemporary representations of their origins. These links are not merely historical curiosities, connections that will conveniently fade into the past, but are very much alive in the conceptions that social science disciplines have of appropriate models and methods of research. Even psychoanalysis, of course, has changed and pluralized itself, with its critical activity often being re-absorbed back into mainstream social sciences.

Many of the key defining characteristics of the social sciences are borrowed from psychoanalysis, and then the psychoanalytic lineage of those ideas lives on hidden in the conceptual and methodological structure of each of the disciplines (Foucault, 1966/1970). Recent anthropological theories of the relationship between 'civilized' and 'savage' mentality, for example, are dependent on the mythical histories of civilization outlined once again by Freud (e.g. Mannoni, 1991). When modern anthropology attempts to distance itself from the linear, Eurocentric and implicitly racist themes in the 'development' of civilization – a progression that is supposed to run from 'animistic' to 'religious' to 'scientific' conceptions of the world – its own alternative structuralist model of the 'savage mind' once again presupposes the existence of the 'unconscious', if now in a different key (e.g. Lévi-Strauss, 1962/1966). Despite common theoretical starting points, such as the incest taboo, structuralist approaches absorbed psychoanalytic approaches into a new form of ethnography. Much participant research and action research is located in the heritage of this transformation of ethnography that still maintained colonialist visions of what were assumed to be 'lesser' cultures.

Sociological theories of the nature of representation, and of the progressive accumulation of cultural resources through which the individual actor becomes internally differentiated, through which the individual becomes 'civilized' as society itself becomes internally differentiated in the course of the transition from close-knit community organization to modern capitalist society, rest upon psychoanalytic conceptions of the relationship between 'pleasure principle' and 'reality principle'. This conception of differentiated social organization then forms the background for analyses of 'representations' of psychoanalysis itself in modern society (e.g. Moscovici, 1976/2008). Even Parsonian functionalist sociology and Meadian interactionist approaches saw direct application of psychoanalytic concepts (Manning, 2005).

Psychology, a discipline which has been most intent on shutting out the existence of past links with psychoanalysis (Burman, 2008a), retains conceptions of the supposed connection between 'frustration' and 'aggression', for example, and then assumes that there is a necessary healthy process that occurs when an individual gratifies their desires. Even in the most normative psychology based on tests and assessment scales (Rorschach, Pfister, Thematic Apperception Test, etc.) research is influenced by psychoanalytic concepts, and the same is true of many 'personality' theories that try to avoid Freud. In recent years, this conception has been evident in the assumption that it is healthy for the individual to share their experiences with others, and this is an assumption that has given a great deal of gratification and self-assurance to qualitative researchers who then can tell themselves and others that the research process itself can be healthy and enlightening to the participants as well as to the researchers and the readers of the reports.

The turn to meaning

The second reason why psychoanalysis must be taken into account in any socio-critical qualitative research is that psychoanalysis has come to structure and inhabit the realm of the social in late capitalist and neoliberal society. This is the case not only in Europe and the United States, where psychoanalysis began and then flowered as an integral part of the development of consumer culture, but also in other parts of the world that are influenced by the political-economic forces of globalization (e.g. Dunker, 2008). Psychoanalytic conceptions of the self – the individual who imagines that there are 'unconscious' reasons for their actions, who suspects that there may be causes in their own childhood for their present-day unhappiness, and who believes that their dreams and slips of the tongue can be interpreted to reveal what they are 'really' thinking – now saturate Western culture (Parker, 1997b).

Historically, we can point to three major conceptual shifts after the Second World War linking the influence of psychoanalysis to the development of capitalism. First, there is participation of psychoanalytic discourse in the rebuilding of the advertising industry in order to produce a new 'culture of desire', a new view of the internal emotional life of the consumer. Second, there is an emerging connection between psychoanalysis and developmental psychology, and so also with a broader rhetoric of progress and development in economy and social theory (Burman, 2008b). Third, there is a massive absorption of psychoanalysis in many forms of psychiatry and in mental health programmes in order to produce new forms of interpretation and regulation of 'abnormality' and suffering. In these three shifts we see a curious coincidence: each shift requires psychoanalysis to produce a kind of qualitative complement to the production of quantitative research data and 'facts' recognizable to positivist investigators. We thus have a process in which there is a re-covering of the 'first nature' of human subjects – biological, objective and material – with a 'second nature' which is psychic, subjective and virtual (Jacoby, 1975). Psychoanalysis thus turns itself from being a radical peripheral and resistant force in early twentieth-century Vienna to being a conformist practice concerned with adapting people to society, a practice that has now spread around the world.

One of the additional reasons why the social sciences now attempt to disavow the early impact of psychoanalytic ideas on their own origins as separate disciplines is that they, the social sciences, are keen to guard their own expertise from contamination by popular culture. Their claims to be able to 'discover' empirical facts that are independent of the immediate consciousness of their research participants and the readers of their reports rest not only upon a division between their own expertise and the false or lacking consciousness of others, but also upon a differentiation of their own forms of knowledge from the explanations that abound in popular culture. Psychoanalysis did not only influence and accompany the social sciences as they each took their first steps to produce knowledge about the world, it also, unlike the social sciences, triumphed in the realm of popular culture, and so that makes it into something that is all the more threatening to 'social scientists' and their own view of the past (Hacking, 1996).

Qualitative research has tended to be obsessed with the spectre of the lack of its own authority. The concept of 'quality' itself requires analysis of phenomena in such a way that there should not really be a reduction to homogeneity, identity and reproducibility, and so, as a consequence, this form of research does not have a guarantee that it is correct. In the case of psychoanalysis, of course, there have been many attempts to fill in this lack of authority with an appeal to the authority of others; institutions like universities or research institutes, state bodies that provide certification or funding, and discursive strategies that facilitate a sacralization of its own specialist vocabulary. There is then the temptation in qualitative research that draws upon psychoanalysis to draw on these external forms of authority to sustain the privileged position they have with respect to those who are also elsewhere outside research institutions.

This threat – and this is the crucial point – is nowhere more potent than in the social sciences concerned with the exploration of *meaning* in qualitative research. While quantitative models and methodologies could pretend to offer a more genuinely 'scientific' account of social relationships and internal mental states than psychoanalysis – which was portrayed as an approach that offered interpretations that could not be numerically validated – the newer qualitative approaches have had to inhabit the same methodological territory as psychoanalysis. In a contemporary culture that suffers the increasing effects of 'psychologization' – in which not only social explanation is reduced to the level of the individual but each individual is invited to believe that their own personal experience contains the key to processes occurring in society (Gordo-López, 2000; Parker, 2007) – qualitative social research neglects psychoanalysis at its peril.

Two points are often made by those attempting to separate psychoanalysis from qualitative research, and these arguments have the effect of privileging psychoanalytic knowledge over other methodological approaches so that it can then be employed within qualitative research. First, there is the argument that psychoanalysis necessarily bring us closer to inner, secret and idiosyncratic meanings. These representations of underlying meanings seem to connect us with a personal 'private language' that can only be translated into a public language in the transference situation and with the support of the psychoanalytic knowledge. In clinical psychoanalysis, the 'transference' describes how the past of the 'analysand' (the patient or client in treatment) is re-enacted and re-experienced in relation to the analyst, and so the clinical practice seems to provide a model for how research outside the clinic should be conducted (a model that we should not, we will argue, take for granted).

The second argument is that meaning can be freely negotiated in terms of a conventional practice between participants in an open conversation, as if it were a form of 'free association'. This free association is the rule of speech that requires that the analysand says everything, however irrelevant or unpleasant, so that this speech can be interpreted by the analyst. Here the real qualities of the meaning are not so dense and fixed, but assumed to be plastic and fluid, and it is often thought to be easy to change and manipulate meaning within an educational or other 'expert' approach. In both arguments, whether there is an appeal to hidden inner meanings or to negotiated conventional meanings, there is the underlying assumption that the construction of meaning is always a successful operation. Meaning can be isolated in fixed contexts and fully described or it can be treated as if it were a positive object like any other object described using particular categories (cf. Kvale, 2003).

However, we would point out that these assumptions that aim to protect psychoanalysis as a specialized form of knowledge are themselves quite mistaken. One might just as well view psychoanalytic investigation as being concerned not with success but with *failure*; psychoanalysis focuses upon absences of meaning, in nonsensical or meaningless experiences. Although qualitative research usually takes meaning to be a positive object, psychoanalysis leads us to consider all of the phenomena that are spoken of from the standpoint of negativity and meaninglessness (Nobus and Quinn, 2005).

Critical engagement

Our argument here is that socio-critical qualitative research needs to engage with psychoanalysis rather than attempt to disavow it, rather than pretend that psychoanalysis does not really already influence the way social scientists work and that therefore it need not be taken seriously. However, we need to be clear about the conceptual grounds of that engagement. It is not because psychoanalysis is a superior mode of explanation, that it provides a better model for research or a methodology that will help us find out 'more' than social scientific research perspectives that attempt to do without psychoanalysis. This is far from the case, and our engagement with psychoanalysis must be configured in such a way that we can appreciate its dangers.

Although we do believe that there are some valuable conceptual resources in psychoanalysis, we see these as arising from the historically embedded position of psychoanalysis rather than from any inherent quality of it as a model or method. Along the road to the disavowal of psychoanalytic discourse there is the idea that if it must be used then it can be 'applied', as if it can be managed as a neutral instrument. The conservative argument against this attempt to apply psychoanalysis is based in the assumption that only 'proper' psychoanalysts should be allowed to do such a thing. This assumption is false, in our view, but this falsity itself contains an important clue as to the social function of psychoanalytic knowledge. The idea that only experts and authentically trained psychoanalysts can deal with its conceptual categories indicates the political nature of the choices the researcher makes when she or he takes on that theoretical framework.

First, the historical legacy of psychoanalysis is a force to be reckoned with today not because psychoanalysis is 'true', but because it has become 'true' for many individuals who explicitly or implicitly structure their own interpretations of personal and social life according to its tenets (that there are unconscious reasons for why they act and that they should share their thoughts about these hidden reasons with others). This 'historical truth' of psychoanalysis can only be tackled by engaging with it and becoming conscious of the force of its underlying assumptions in the texture of social life. This link between psychoanalysis and 'popular knowledge' was pointed out many times in the history of the approach (e.g. Freud, 1933). Examples include the way Freud takes the side of popular culture against 'scientific' conceptions to insist that dreams have meaning, the way 'conversion' from mental to physical in a hysterical symptom is seen as determined by the commonly understood view someone has about their body rather than a neurological description, and the way psychoanalytic treatment develops through the vocabulary chosen by the analysand rather than in the discourse of the analyst.

Second, the present-day effects of psychoanalysis are particularly potent among social scientists, especially those involved in qualitative research because they believe that it is more important – even that it is 'liberating' – to study meaning instead of producing numerical representations of the world. The Marxist argument that those who do not learn from history are condemned to repeat it is nowhere more pertinent than with respect to those who try to pretend that psychoanalysis is of no relevance to them. If the dead weight of the past is indeed to be thrown off as people engage in socio-critical qualitative research, that process can only occur if we know what it is we are throwing off. The question turns back once again to the point at which psychoanalytic frameworks were imported into the social sciences. In theoretical domains we find that this process of importation is often the diametric opposite of what happens in 'normal' capitalist economic exchange. When we buy something we often have the impression that we end up with *less* than what we meant or expected to get. The problem with conceptual importation – such as that of psychoanalysis into academic disciplines – is that we always get *more* than we intended to buy into. This means that even when we try to evacuate the disciplines of psychoanalytic concepts we still find that 'surplus' remaining, and it structures the knowledge that is left behind.

Four psychoanalytic instances

Now we can turn to particular aspects of psychoanalysis as a worldview (as a 'model'), and as a mode of reasoning (as a 'method'). We do, incidentally, follow Freud's (1933) argument that psychoanalytic methodology should not be turned into a worldview, but should operate in relation to science, here social science. We will show in more detail, through examining the insidious operation of psychoanalytic categories in social scientific research, how it might be possible to develop socio-critical approaches that transcend commonsensical ideological psychoanalytic conceptions of the world. Through these four instances we will illustrate the general argument that a progressive alternative to the usual procedures of disavowal with respect to psychoanalysis that obtain in the social sciences can be elaborated.

We have deliberately used the psychoanalytic term 'disavowal' – a strategy of denial alongside simultaneous instrumental use of what is denied – with its resonances of refusal and fixation, of the attempt to shut away something and the corresponding fetishization of that which comes to stand in the place of that which is shut away. In classical psychoanalysis 'disavowal' is meant to describe how the child might refuse to acknowledge that they can see no penis on the mother's body, and fix on another object to replace that absent thing to create a fetish through which they can pretend that there is no real difference between men and women. We are, of course, using the notion of disavowal in a much more formal sense (that is without the naked mother, child's perception and absent penis as necessary contents of the structure), to describe how denial that something is the case (that psychoanalysis is a powerful structuring force in the social sciences, for example) covers over the value still secretly given to that something, or something that stands in for psychoanalysis (Laplanche and Pontalis, 1988).

The structuring principle we will use to describe these four instances is that one of the most important consequences of the shutting out of psychoanalysis – the attempt by the social sciences to pretend that it is of no importance – is that psychoanalytic conceptions of meaning then return in a distorted, fetishized form. They return both as repetitions from the history of the development of the social sciences and as material from psychologized popular culture that is saturated with psychoanalytic categories. The process of engagement with these instances of psychoanalysis in qualitative research then requires a 'working through' that will accomplish the 'sublation' of distorted fetishized elements of psychoanalysis. A 'sublation' here is used to capture the way in which we intend to refuse the commonsensical and ideological psychoanalytic categories we will describe and to rework and to improve the aspects of them that should be retained for genuinely progressive socio-critical qualitative research.

In the history of philosophy a certain idea is dominant in a certain period and then, after a time, the idea fades in significance, a principle is found to be false, or the problem is resolved and attention is then focused on new problems (Kuhn, 1962). The concept of 'sublation' captures the way that the old idea or principle is not usually simply disproved and disposed of but is maintained, contained in the new higher-level principle that has replaced it. As another example (which is conceptualized by Piagetian and Vygotskian theorists in developmental psychology as well as by those drawing on psychoanalytic ideas), in our childhood we wrestle with certain problems which are forgotten by the time we are adults, but in fact it is those very struggles which have formed us as the adult that we now are, no longer troubled by those same problems. Thus sublation is at work, superseding but simultaneously preserving what is apparently cancelled out (Bottomore, 1991; Bensaïd, 2002).

Sublation of each of the four instances, then, enables us to produce conceptual models and methods that are simultaneously explicitly indebted to the conceptual and cultural history of psychoanalysis and, at the same time rigorously and deliberately '*anti-psychoanalytic*'. Notice, however, that this 'anti-psychoanalysis' should not proceed by way of simple evasion or denouncement; it should be accomplished in such a way as to avoid secretly maintaining presuppositions, of what we had attempted to evade, or to repeat, in reverse, the modes of argument of the position we defined ourselves against as we denounced it. We do not want to end up like the atheist who spends all their time denouncing God, whose existence is then still defined by the God that obsesses them.

The hold of psychoanalysis on culture and on the subjects who comprise it requires a more interpretive (dare we say 'psychoanalytic') strategy. For these particular purposes – to develop socio-critical qualitative research in the social sciences – it is necessary to find a new way of dealing with and dispensing with psychoanalysis, but we will see that it is only possible if we approach that task with due acknowledgement of the historical weight of psychoanalysis upon our present-day conceptual strategies. Let us now turn to the four psychoanalytic instances.

Interpretation

Social scientists turning to qualitative research are often able to acknowledge that the 'interpretative' stance they adopt is cognate with, if not influenced to some degree by, psychoanalysis. The 'interpretive turn' in the social sciences already calls upon a quasi-psychoanalytic sensitivity in which there is a 'suspicion' of the first, immediate, surface layer of the research material – whether that is an ethnographic account, interview transcript or cultural text – and an attempt to delve beneath to something that will explain what is 'really' going on (cf. Rorty, 1980). There are two aspects of this interpretive activity which are particularly problematic and which owe a great deal to the impact of psychoanalytic ideology inside and outside the social sciences.

The first aspect is the implication that in some way the research material – which the analyst sometimes likes, in deference to quantitative research paradigms perhaps, to call the 'data' – is the mere 'manifest' content. If it makes sense to the participant as they produce it in an interview or as they describe what they are doing in an ethnographic study, the reasoning goes, then we must be all the more suspicious of what the underlying hidden meanings are. The avoidance of an appeal to authorial intention to explain the meaning of a text in the case of discursive or other interpretative readings of cultural material rests on the same assumption: that it would be pointless and fruitless to ask an author why they produced the text we have before us – and so it is as if only the researcher can detect the real reason. It is not that this argument is in itself wrong; rather it serves to emphasize the point that we must ask what assumptions are brought to bear when we view it as a mistake to go to the author to get closer to the 'real' meaning. As a kind of complementary myth, it is sometimes thought that we can fix meaning in a clear and exhaustive corpus of text with delimitated boundaries and so put a halt to the flux of meaning. In either case – the autonomy of the author or the autonomy of the corpus – we are prisoners of the fiction of 'real' meaning even at the moment we try to avoid it.

It is, in the standard social scientific approach to the research material, tempting to excavate the 'real' meaning, as if it were the 'latent' content that already existed beneath the surface, as if it were a dream text (Freud, 1900/1999). Needless to say, the various procedures by which the social scientist thinks they are able to reveal the 'latent' content rely upon an expertise that is not available to those who produce the accounts in the first place. Immediately a position is adopted which resonates with and reproduces the worst banalized representations of the psychoanalyst peering into the mind behind the jumble of free associations and rationalizations that have been offered by the poor, unwitting, speaking subject. This operation is based on the idea that psychoanalytic interpretation functions as a translation process in which we first have the natural, ambiguous and confused language of the subject and we then translate it into the artificial, unequivocal and clear language of the researcher.

An appropriate tactical engagement with this assumption, which is at one with the broader strategic argument we are elaborating here, is to refuse the lure of *meaning* as such. Instead of buying into the underlying assumption that our task is to excavate meaning and to produce a richer, more detailed meaning – whether that is 'thick description' that goes beyond what any informant told us or 'close reading' that reveals underlying themes – we suggest that we take an immediately 'anti-psychoanalytic' step to *reduce* the degree of meaning in the interpretations we produce. It is possible here to mobilize elements of ideology-critique from the Russian formalists, for example, and to reduce the 'meanings' that seem so self-evident to the researcher and reader to nonsense, and through this 'estrangement' effect to start to examine how the nonsensical elements function (Bennett, 1979; Nobus and Quinn, 2005).

In this perspective, interpretation functions as a kind of transcription or transliteration, rather than as a translation. A transcription goes from one level of expression (spoken language, images and gestures, for example) to another level of expression (in a written language, for example). A transliteration goes from one system of writing to another (from Chinese to English, for example). When we are able to recognize that we have a huge problem when we record an interview and then transcribe it into written discourse, when we pay radical attention to the choices, exclusions and decisions we have to make in this process, we can take a distance from the tempting principle of full 'positive meaning'. There are therefore many procedures that we undertake automatically in qualitative research that we have to put into question when we refuse the 'interpretative' paradigm; we have to question the existence of perfect translation, our confidence in synonyms, the natural contiguity of certain expressions, and the efficiency of communication as a whole.

Interiority

A strong temptation in social scientific research is to attempt to delve inside the mind of the individual subject, to discover what their beliefs are about social processes or to unearth their 'feelings' about social relationships. This temptation was strong enough in the quantitative tradition, and was present not only in psychology – which is devoted to the study of internal mental processes – but also in cognitive and experiential versions of anthropology and sociology. The attempt to focus on 'feelings', rather than words and discourses, mires us once again in the presumption that there could be such a thing as perfect communication. The search for feelings brings in its train assumptions about reciprocity and reflexivity, and these assumptions function as an index of a supposed identity of the meaning. Empathy and spontaneity are then elevated into what are taken to be natural virtues of the qualitative researcher.

The turn to qualitative research in the social sciences comes at a time when psychologization in culture has increased to such an extent that the meanings that an individual subject attaches to phenomena are often assumed to provide the touchstone of truth. In place of traditional notions of 'validity' and 'reliability', the intuitive warrant for the value of interpretations has come to rest upon the assumed correspondence between what the reader, researcher and research participant really 'think' or 'feel' to be the case (e.g. Ellis and Bochner, 2000). Such emotional criteria, which work so well in everyday life for sure, can be very unhelpful in qualitative research. It fits with the argument, sometimes to be found in psychoanalytic writing, to the effect that 'repression' bears upon affect rather than representations (e.g. Freud, 1927). Actually affects could be clarified in more detail in everyday conversation when we have a partner who does *not* comprehend them perfectly, but who questions the way they function, and this questioning is what we should be encouraging in qualitative research.

The assumption that there is an 'interior' realm of the mind that must be brought into the light of day also corresponds, of course, to popularized versions of psychoanalysis. Even some versions of psychoanalytic theory and practice after Freud have rested on the assumption that the human mind is a kind of space which is filled with conscious and unconscious 'contents' which can be retrieved by a clinician or researcher with the right skills (cf. Leader, 2000). In this way the banalized and distorted notion of 'interpretation' – the supposed translation of hidden latent meanings into the manifest content described by the psychoanalytically oriented social scientist – is accompanied by the equally banal notion that psychoanalysis concerns itself with secret contents inside the mind. The principle of affective identification between the researcher and their object of investigation must instead be challenged, replaced with a principle of *unfamiliarity*, by which we try to localize what is strange in apparently familiar taken-for-granted meaning.

Our response to this problem of interiority, as a strategic engagement that works with it in order to unravel its presuppositions, is that we should refuse the opposition between exteriority and interiority, and that we can treat what is putatively 'interior' as being constructed and maintained through the operation of social processes. It is the very operation of these social processes in capitalist society that serves to encourage each individual to imagine that mental phenomena are inside their minds in the first place rather than outside (Parker, 2007). However, rather than turning to quasi-behaviourist notions of the determination of individual subjects by social circumstances, it is the particular construction of the interior that we wish to question. Study of 'interiority' thus also requires study of processes of psychologization perhaps at some moments as a form of ideology. This does not mean avoiding the emotional dimension of research but it does mean considering emotion not in terms of inner interior experience, or as an external observable behaviour, but as a *practice*. Here again are productive effects of a refusal of the received opposition between latent and manifest content.

Subjectivity

The attempt to delve inside the mind of a research participant is matched by the attempt by the researcher to delve inside their own mind in order to bring out any 'biases' or 'prejudices' they might have. There is a long tradition in anthropology and sociology, particularly in ethnographic forms of research, to account for the effects of the intervention of the researcher (e.g. Clifford and Marcus, 1986). The fact that a particular individual or team is entering the field and describing it from the vantage point of a particular institution will have immense effects not only on the forms of description, but also often on the research participants themselves as they puzzle about what they do and try to make it meaningful to the outsiders. Our problem is not with this questioning of institutional positions and the privilege accorded to those in universities, but with the way the problem is configured when it starts to be inhabited by psychoanalytic notions. The usual way of conceptualizing the response of the analyst as 'counter-transference' feeds this orientation to research subjectivity (e.g. Freud, 1915; Hollway, 1989).

When there is undue concern with the 'subjectivity' of the researcher they then come to understand the work of 'reflexivity' as entailing the search inside their own mind for hidden motives for the choice of research topic or interpretations they make of it. This reflexivity is often reduced to the individual 'subjective' decisions the researcher makes, rather than treating reflexivity as a function of institutional positions and collectively maintained requirements (Parker, 2005). When we look to these particular 'subjective' elements we find rather poor research; to be 'subjective' often means not much more than general identifications or unjustified decisions, and an appeal to the 'subjective' as such is commonly used to close discussion down rather than open it up.

Our response to this problem is to refuse the opposition between objectivity and subjectivity, and show how the realm of the subjective inhabits even those practices that are usually thought to be objective. Here we draw on arguments from within feminism, Marxist theory and post-structuralist critique that illustrate how the claim to 'objectivity' calls upon a series of elaborate procedures that reflect certain standpoints (e.g. Henriques *et al.*, 1984/1998). Close analysis of the way subjectivity is manufactured in relation to different forms of technology also serves to demystify the realm of the personal as something that is usually pitted against the political realm (Gordo-López and Cleminson, 2004). It is more important to show how subjectivity and objectivity is produced in certain language games and to ask what the stakes of the opposition between subjectivity and objectivity are, rather than delving into one side of the equation abstracted from the other.

Relationships

The domain between research participant and researcher – between the 'interiority' of the object of research and the 'subjectivity' of the agent – is of crucial importance in qualitative social science. Once again, this domain is prone to psychologization and in particular to the unbidden influence of psychoanalytic conceptions of 'relationships', which are now often configured as painful and difficult 'research relationships'. Psychoanalytic notions are often apparent in the language used to describe these relationships, sometimes in the use of the terms 'painful' and 'difficult' employed in their therapeutic senses – that is, as mentally or emotionally painful and difficult – and in the way the institutional relationships between researchers and researched are often described as structured by 'boundaries' that should be maintained and honoured.

There is then a temptation for the researcher to try to protect the research participant and respect the putative 'boundaries', and thus to infantilize the research participant. In this way the 'painful' and 'difficult' experiences the researcher has concerning the relationship – a relationship that is already at this point being described using popular therapeutic terminology – are also attributed to the research participant, and a series of protective procedures, which go under the name of 'accountability', 'confidentiality' and 'ethics', are put in place. This is a state of affairs we characterize as 'generalized transference'; that is, the specific language of the clinic is used to apply to every social relationship, here to research relationships. Here again there is the danger of extrapolating from clinical psychoanalysis, which itself has too often been treated as a privileged domain in which general relational phenomena are assumed to operate (cf. Freud, 1915).

Here we find some complex extensions of the idea of method as such. Method is a sequence of paths the researcher, or someone else who is in the same position, could follow without taking any personal risk or choice in order to produce replicable knowledge. The formulation of a clear, replicable sequence provides what pretends to be a guarantee, but it also suggests that if you choose a method you are no longer responsible for its consequences; the researcher simply elects to follow a 'method' and then faithfully obeys it. Qualitative research, on the other hand, is not so easily protected by the anonymity of the method, and so there has emerged a new series of tactics by which to neutralize the inherent risk of the practice of method. These require extracting from the research situation any form of conflict, pain and potential suffering that may obtain in the encounter between researcher and research participant. This pacifies all parties, and invites them to believe that they do not have to think about their activities or the effects of the research intervention.

This problem can only be confronted by detailed historical study of how the clinic, and forms of subjectivity that occur inside this peculiar social mechanism that is designed to produce 'transference', are constituted (Dunker, 2010). The only way the apparatus of clinical psychoanalysis can be tackled is to 'relativize' it; that is, to render the transference into something specific rather than pretending that it is a necessary characteristic of all relationships that must then necessarily be attended to by social scientists. This means turning from generic rules and anonymity of the researcher to taking seriously the particular responsibility that bears upon someone embarking on activities and producing effects that the researcher cannot know about in their entirety before the research takes place.

Socio-critical strategies

Some readers will detect the traces of psychoanalysis in the very strategies we have used to unmask it. To this accusation our response is that you should not confuse smuggling (if you suspect us of importing more of the contraband material we declared and ditched at the door) with tactical deployment. If, for example, the reduction of 'meaning' to 'nonsense' in an interpretative procedure that attempts to avoid psychoanalytic ideology in psychologized culture ends up being close to what some psychoanalysts claim they actually do in their own clinical practice, then so be it. That is not our problem; our task is to tackle the immediate impact of psychoanalytic reasoning in social science. The same point applies to the argument that psychoanalysts themselves deconstruct the opposition between interiority and exteriority (Miller, 1986), and that they treat subjectivity as a function of transference pertaining to the clinic (Nasio, 1998). Again, we are happy to have these writers from within psychoanalysis on board as allies in the argument we are making here.

Psychoanalysis does provide some useful resources, but the ideological aspects, sedimented in popular culture through the banalization and recuperation of the ideas to make them compatible with contemporary psychologization, need to be carefully worked through and 'sublated' so that what is progressive can be retained and elaborated for further critical work. These strategies are not procedures that, once applied, can then be forgotten or taken for granted, and this is why we have refrained from giving prescriptions for how to develop psychoanalysis as a 'method' based on its own particular 'model' of social relations (or even an 'example' that would pin it down). Any method must be constructed from the particular qualities of the situation under examination. There is always an element of risk, and the decisions we take cannot be guaranteed by rules and procedures or ethics committees. If the object of inquiry resists the method we bring to bear, it is surely better that the object rather than the method survives at the end of the process (Latour, 2000; Kvale, 2003).

The stance that we have taken is to refuse the strategy of 'disavowal' that intensifies the power of the enemy substance – psychoanalysis – when it is fetishized and turned into something that becomes more dangerous than it actually was because of what we have done to ourselves during the construction of our own defences against it. The enemy to good research functions thus because of the peculiar kind of grip it has on our work. It would be possible to find among the precursors to our task the work of those who attempted to work through and slough off what was 'abstract' about the procedures of psychoanalytic interpretation and to retain a practice that was 'concrete' (Politzer, 1994; for a psychoanalytic rebuttal of these arguments, see Laplanche and Leclaire, 1972).

Actually, most of the qualitative research directly or indirectly inspired by psychoanalysis turns psychoanalysis into a kind of abstract psychology, with the exact characteristics pointed out by Georges Politzer (1994): a presumption of the conventionality of meaning (of categories, judgements and contracts between researcher and their 'subjects'), atomization of meaning and behaviour (and the classification of 'attitudes'), the attempt to deal with mental process instead of actual 'life drama' (with an attendant affective dimension and the premise of total communication), an attempt to sidestep change (or 'interference' in the life of the 'object' under study), and the absence of any reflection about the historicity of meaning and the historical location of the researcher in certain assumptions about what problems and solutions pertain to a particular situation.

Psychoanalysis has many times in its history been defined as an anti-psychology (e.g. Burman, 2008a). If we aim to generate, experimentally, an 'anti-psychoanalytic' approach, perhaps we may arrive at an 'anti-anti-psychology'; in other words, at a way of encountering the nature of subjectivity in contemporary society. In this way, an approach to the individual that psychology as a discipline usually betrays connects with the broader domain of the social sciences.

It could be said that we have aimed at a 'deconstruction' of psychoanalysis, in such a way as to question the imbrication of its ideological superstructure with strategies of discipline or confession (Hook, 2007). Our analysis has required a sensitivity to the historically mediated role of psychoanalysis, that treats it as an ideological form that calls for interpretation so that it may better be harnessed to processes of change; this dialectical analysis of what is 'rational' in psychoanalysis is also, in some ways, indebted to Marxism. The standpoint we have taken is also very much influenced by feminist arguments about human nature as historically mediated and appropriate epistemological procedures that attend to how social reality is configured so that those who benefit from it assume that this is the way the world is and must be.

There are clearly serious contradictions between psychoanalytic, post-structuralist, Marxist and feminist approaches in the social sciences, and we have not intended to privilege psychoanalysis, merely to focus on what it promises (Dunker, 2010). We anticipate that the research process will be reinvented each time a qualitative social scientist begins their work, and particular potent psychoanalytic instances must be anticipated and refused as necessary, sublated as the work proceeds. Then it is also Lacanian.

5   Lacanian ethics in psychology

Seven paradigms

This chapter is concerned with Lacanian perspectives on research in psychology, with a specific focus on ethics. It takes another step forward from the discussion of qualitative research in the previous chapter. The field of 'ethics' in the discipline is one of the most fraught areas of debate for researchers, and critical psychologists carrying out qualitative research have many times been confronted with obstacles to their work by 'ethics committees' which are often made up of colleagues from the old paradigm laboratory-experimental tradition who seem unable to comprehend what it is they are supposed to be evaluating.

We see here that different competing, and often implicit, notions of ethics in psychology are very different from those that are elaborated in philosophy and in Lacanian debate. The chapter argues that we can find seven paradigms in and against 'psychological' ethics in the Lacanian tradition. The first three are problematic paradigms identified by Lacan (on the good as an ideal, on conformity with moral law, and on the distribution of goods); the fourth (on democratic openness), fifth (on desire) and sixth (on the act) are possible ethical alternatives that have been read into Lacan; and the seventh (fidelity to the event) is developed at greater length here from Lacan's work in the field of political theory by Alain Badiou. The chapter considers how these paradigms question psychology, and what the lures are for psychologists in these paradigms.

The chapter therefore functions not only as a review of paradigms of 'ethics' in psychology, but also as an introduction to the contribution of Badiou. The point here is not only that Badiou takes forward Lacanian arguments in and against the discipline of psychology. It is that 'Lacanian psychoanalysis' is a field of debate in which there are a variety of different theoretical positions.

'Ethics' is something that psychology nowadays has become much preoccupied with, but the attempts by the discipline to enforce ethical behaviour have only served to bind its practitioners all the more firmly to the dubious practices that it was founded upon (Parker, 2005; Neill, 2015). Here, in contrast, I want to explore some critical theoretical vantage points on ethics in psychology from the standpoint of ethics in Lacanian psychoanalysis (Lacan, 1986). Perhaps it is possible to discover in Lacan some specifications for ethics. Perhaps the chapter will lead us in this direction. But before we embark on that course, it is worth rehearsing what Lacan provides in terms of critique (Johnstone, 2001). In my view, this is what Lacan is useful for; despite complaints about Lacan's elliptical style, we actually find some conceptual clarification in his writing of what we are up against in ethics, and so what we are up against in so-called 'ethics' in psychology.

Let us start with the three paradigms Lacan worries away at (Lacan, 1986; Rajchman, 1991). They are paradigms with a good pedigree, but they actually come a little too close to mainstream models in psychology.

The first paradigm is one that presumes that we can all agree what a 'Good' is that we should be aiming at and against which we can easily define what falls below it as the ideal standard. This is a notion of ethics that we find in Aristotle onwards. There are, of course, theoretical frameworks in the discipline of psychology that would be compatible with this notion of the Good and of ethics. Specifications of essential underlying human nature, perhaps deriving from the secular humanist tradition, for example, would presume that we do know what it is to do right and wrong. The problem is that once we start to take psychoanalysis seriously the perception of the Good is thrown into question. The Good is not something that already exists somewhere to be intuited and aimed at, but it is something that is constructed by us. First because it functions as an ideal which we set up ourselves based on our own idiosyncratic experience of what is delightful and alluring to us, an image of what we would like to be or a point from which we would like to seen as likeable. And second because every notion of the Good that we too easily conflate with what is beautiful to us is suffused with fantasy. What may be good to us as an ideal that is suffused with fantasy, then, may turn out to be quite horrific to other people.

The second paradigm appeals to an imperative to follow the right course of action, which we assume to be potentially if not actually present in each individual human being. This is the way of Kant, and the categorical imperative, in which we are asked to assess our action according to the maxim that we should imagine it to be carried out by all other human beings, applicable to them; this maxim is designed to bring some measure of universality directly into the moral decision-making of any particular individual. Again, this is an ethical paradigm that we can imagine certain traditions in psychology adopting with ease. The image of the person as containing within themselves a conscience by virtue of which they are able to participate in a society as a civilized, enlightened human being can then even be translated into certain psychoanalytic models of the personality that are included in psychology.

The problem with this paradigm, which operates according to some notion of the existence of conscience under law, is that some people who carry out the most horrific actions do feel themselves to be following some version of a moral injunction and to be in conformity with what human nature is like.

The third paradigm is concerned with the calculation of goods, of costs and benefits of actions for different individuals. This is the universe of Jeremy Bentham, which presumes that it is possible to determine what will be good for people and bad for them and to arrange roles and responsibilities so that the greatest possible good is distributed among them. Again, psychology includes enough models of human behaviour to warrant this version of ethics. Here, some of the strands of work in the behaviourist tradition, which seem to refuse to adopt a specific moral standpoint, do actually rest on notions of what healthy and unhealthy patterns of behaviour are and how contingencies of reinforcement might be set up to bring benefit to people.

The problem with this paradigm is that it rather conveniently overlooks, as does behaviourism, what the stakes are for the individuals or groups that arrange the distribution of goods. Some neutral position outside the system is presupposed so that decisions can be made which are not themselves affected by certain benefits. Psychoanalysis, which is one of the most intense reflexive conceptual frameworks, would ask what the individual who arranges things gets out of it. And the problem lies not so much at the level of particular decisions as at a deeper systemic level – structurally distributed powers – in the very position accorded to those who will decide.

Lacan's discussion of these first three paradigms for ethics is a groundclearing exercise. It is not possible to do psychoanalysis if you operate on some ideal image of the Good, if you intend to strengthen conscience and conformity, or if you try to calculate the costs and benefits of actions. Versions of psychoanalysis that have degenerated into forms of psychology might be satisfied with these options, but Lacanian psychoanalysis requires a distance from these ideas, and some distance from psychological notions of ethics. So this raises the question as to where there is some positive content to a Lacanian specification of ethics. Let us turn to three paradigms that have been elaborated as alternatives in readings of Lacan. They do not sit easily with psychology, but that is not reason enough for those of us doing critical work in qualitative research in psychology to adopt them.

One possibility as a fourth paradigm, then, is that the very uncertainty and indeterminacy of ethical grounds for action should be understood and grasped as that, as uncertain and indeterminate grounds. Discussions of 'democracy' in the Lacanian tradition have often taken this position. It is also an argument made, for example, by Laclau and Mouffe (1985) in their argument for 'radical democracy' as a 'post-Marxist' politics, and elaborated in detail by Stavrakakis (1999). The ground-clearing work of Lacan would then be work to be undertaken again and again by each individual subject.

Another possibility, our fifth paradigm, is that one should take seriously the role of desire as characteristic and determinative of what it is to be a human being. One also often finds among Lacanians a fixation on the phrase from Lacan's Seminar VII, *The Ethics of Psychoanalysis*, that 'the only thing of which one can be guilty is of having given ground relative to one's desire' (Lacan, 1986/1992: 319). The way this is sometimes posed makes it seem like there is some kind of ethical imperative to follow one's desire, and we would then be led to ask whether giving ground on one's desire would be unethical.

A sixth paradigm, attractive to some readers of Lacan, is to look to some authentic 'act' as the ethical instance. The figure around whom this motif is condensed is Antigone. When Antigone refuses to obey the order that her brother should not be given a decent burial and insists on going to perform rites of mourning on the body despite the fact that she knows very well that she will herself be condemned to death if she does so, she is engaging in an extreme 'act' to remain true to her desire which changes the symbolic coordinates of the situation. This heroic act is most thoroughly individualized in the writings of Slavoj Žižek (e.g. Žižek, 1999; cf. Butler, 2000).

What is problematic about these three alternatives is that they risk a reduction to the realm of the individual: as participants in a democracy who together decompose and produce a transient order that can be dissolved by an open 'radical democratic' process; as desiring subjects commanded not to give way on their desire; or as exemplary figures who go to the limits and cross them in order to hold to what they believe is right (Parker, 2004). So, is it possible to embed Lacan's critique of dominant ethical paradigms in politics? We now turn to a seventh paradigm.

Alain Badiou, in a book first published in French in 1998 and then in English in 2001 titled *Ethics: An Essay on the Understanding of Evil*, develops a critique of dominant paradigms in ethics and sets out some coordinates for rethinking what the relation is between ethics and evil (Badiou, 1998/2001). Badiou is not a Lacanian, and has no interest in psychoanalysis as a form of therapy, but he does take Lacan as a key reference point in philosophy when Badiou says that his 'theory is that philosophy should always think as closely as possible to antiphilosophy' (Badiou, 1998/2001: 122). Although Badiou has particular worries about the way 'anti-philosophy' too often functions to close off serious reflection, we can take this proposal as an invitation to think through his proposals in relation to anti-psychology.

Against the (first) position on ethics derived from Aristotle, Badiou is concerned with the way that appeals to 'ethics' do not usually open up thinking about what an ethical course of action might be and with the way that assumptions about the 'Good' close things down. He argues that 'The ethical conception of man, besides the fact that its foundation is either biological (images of victims) or "Western" (the self-satisfaction of the armed benefactor), prohibits every broad, positive vision of possibilities' (Badiou, 1998/2001: 14). This argument also neatly captures the dead end that we arrive at when we simply pit the positivist laboratory-experimental tradition in psychology against the more humanistic versions of psychology in qualitative research that aims to investigate and respect the meanings people give to their actions. This forced choice leads us into a view of those we research as objects, and an implicit assumption that they are victims of biological or behavioural processes or of them as self-actualizing agents who will benefit from enlightenment as to their capacities. The latter position, which is more tempting today among critical psychologists, leads to beneficial interventions in line with a version of a 'prime directive' (in which local laws are honoured).

These problems also apply to the second paradigm we outlined, that deriving from Kant. There is a further point to be made here, however, with respect to the way we imagine others following the same moral procedures as ourselves. The 'categorical imperative', as a maxim that demands mutual recognition of others who are assumed to act according to the same precepts, entails that we know or imagine what those others are like and that we know or imagine that we are like them. Badiou points out that this 'recognition' of others as a basis for ethics is very problematic, and he argues that 'the whole ethical production based upon recognition of the other should be purely and simply abandoned' (Badiou, 1998/2001: 25). The reason is that an overall rule requires homogenization of cultural historical experience: 'this celebrated "other" is acceptable only if he is a *good* other – which is to say what, exactly, if not *the same as us*?' (Badiou, 1998/2001: 24)

This usefully draws attention to the pitfalls of humanistic approaches within qualitative research that are predicated on 'recognition' of others as the solution to all ethical dilemmas. Qualitative research that rests on in-depth interviewing often makes the mistake of imagining that 'rapport' between interviewer and interviewee indicates that there is a shared frame of reference and mutual respect. These approaches then assume that the process is 'ethical'. They always smuggle in some idea about what those others are like so that we respect them on our terms and then sanctify that conditional respect with the word 'ethics'.

There is also a powerful warning in Badiou's work against the ethics derived from Bentham. This warning goes beyond the problem that some position must be presupposed above or outside the system of costs and benefits. Badiou draws attention to the even more dangerous consequences that may follow from respecting 'good' others and treating all the good others as part of the same community as ourselves. This is exactly where the homogenizing of a collection of subjects as a 'community' turns into the 'totalizing' of their experience as a 'truth' which will then be imposed upon them as a condition for recognizing them as part of the community. As Badiou puts it, 'the community and the collective are the unnamables of political truth: every attempt "politically" to name a community induces a disastrous Evil' (Badiou, 1998/2001: 86). Qualitative research likes to be open to shared meaning, but it also needs to attend to the contradictions between different systems of meaning. The appeal to a 'community' in recent 'critical psychology' is one all-too-convenient way of sealing over the contradictions between participants, and as with all so-called 'ethical' procedures in psychological research, the story serves to satisfy the outsider and those inside who benefit from that story (because it reproduces the position of power they enjoy).

Badiou does not presume that Evil is primary and that ethical activity has to be forged out of a struggle with it. This is important, for that conception of ethics – in which we assume that people will do the worse unless they are prevented from doing so – operates as a bedrock assumption for most attempts to specify what ethics should be. Most dominant approaches to ethics today combine that view, that people will do Evil, with an attempt to shore up a law or set of procedures that will ensure that they know what the Good is; the promoter of ethics thus aims to reinforce the law and make it so that each individual embeds that law in their own conscience. This is the basis that most ethics committees in psychology operate on. It is not accidental that an assumption about conscience in conformity with the law – the assumption derived from the Kantian (second) paradigm we discussed above – should be combined with a view of Evil as a starting point in human action, for there is actually warrant for this position in Kant himself. Towards the end of his life Kant toyed with the possibility that there was some primary 'radical Evil' that preceded a choice for the Good in man. (It is worth holding on to that specification of 'man' as the subject for a moment, for it draws attention to the role of feminist critical work on ethics.)

With respect to the three possible readings of prescription for an alternative ethical standpoint that one might find in Lacan (paradigms four, five and six), Badiou offers some useful ways of thinking about those options. Democracy, desire and the act are things that signal the openness of human possibilities, and what is important about each of them is that they presuppose that we cannot know in advance all of the parameters and all of the consequences; so Badiou's take on the reference to 'desire' in Lacan is also a way of opening up the question of uncertainty and of choice in human action. In his reading, '"do not give up on your desire" rightly means: "do not give up on that part of yourself that you do not know"' (Badiou, 1998/2001: 47). So what, according to Badiou, can we know?

Badiou works with a kind of conceptual grid in which we are able to conceptualize the different spheres in which ethics is treated as fidelity to an event, and in which a truth and subject appears. He writes: 'I shall call "truth" (*a* truth) the real process of a fidelity to an event: and which this fidelity *produces* in the situation' (Badiou, 1998/2001: 42). This is not an overall scheme for ethics, but a distinctive way of thinking about what ethics might be in different domains of human activity; for Badiou, 'Ethics does not exist. There is only the *ethic-of* (of politics, of love, of science, of art)' (Badiou, 1998/2001: 28). Let us to turn to these four spheres – politics, love, science and art – and the different ways in which that ethics is dissolved and Evil appears – as simulacrum, betrayal or totalization.

If we take the sphere of politics first we can see the way that this conceptual grid works. Take the example of the October Revolution in Russia in 1917. The fidelity to that event as an overthrow of capitalism and the construction of a socialist democratic order based on soviet power calls into being a certain kind of 'truth' in which the continuation of militant solidarity with the revolution retroactively names it as being exemplary of a certain historical moment and possibility. It names it as such after the event because the Bolsheviks did not know at the time that this would be the October Revolution as a singular event appearing on the scene of world history in the way it did; 'in the end, a truth *changes the names* of elements in the situation' (Badiou, 1998/2001: 82). There are three ways that Evil appears against this event.

The first – the case of simulacrum and terror – would be, for example, in the rise of Nazism. The National Socialists borrowed symbols from the communist movement, presented themselves as a popular workers' movement and staged a political 'revolution' to save German capitalism, seizure of power that deliberately evoked the Bolshevik revolution. This was, of course, only one of the faces of Nazism, but insofar as it cast itself in the image of socialist revolution it functioned as a 'simulacrum' of the Russian revolution. One might imagine other events that function in this way, and the extent to which the crushing of Kronstadt by the Bolsheviks in 1921 was a 'defence' of the revolution against counter-revolutionaries or a moment of terror against brave workers as a simulacrum of the revolution is a political question. Different traditions in and outside the Left debate it. How one positions oneself in relation to specific events during the years of degeneration into Stalinism after 1917 entails the production of a certain kind of naming of the process, fidelity to the event of 1917 that was betrayed by Stalin and the production of certain 'truth' and a certain 'subject' (revolutionary socialists, Left oppositionists, Trotskyists). As far as Badiou is concerned, 'it is only a commitment to a truth-process that "*induces* a subject"' (Hallward, 2001: xxvi).

The second way in which Evil appears is through betrayal. Again, the conceptualization of betrayal here does not specify what the correct course of action is. A historical content cannot be directly read off from this account of ethics. Precisely the opposite, for it is a question of argument in which there is a contest of different political accounts mobilizing different forms of truth. What 'betrayal' points to here is the cowardly or cynical abandonment of what one knows to be a truth. What Badiou has in mind here when he discusses betrayal in the field of politics is the shift to the centre or right by ex-Leftists who declare that they now realize the error of their ways. The fidelity to the event, and corresponding forms of subjective truth, are given up; but worse, there is a turning against that truth.

The third form of Evil is when there is a totalitarian imposition of the truth of an event as universal model, incontestable and fixed. What I referred to just now as the 'betrayal' of Stalin in the crystallization of the police bureaucracy in the Soviet Union would more accurately be framed in terms of totalization of the truth so that it turns into its reverse. This what Badiou refers as 'absolutization' of truth, and he argues that 'Every absolutization of the power of truth organizes an Evil' (Badiou, 1998/2001: 84). For example, one's fidelity to the event is turned into a coerced, homogenized version of history in the service of a power that must systematically erase memory of what the democratic opening of the Bolshevik revolution entailed. And it is here that the appeal to 'community' can be a way of shutting down possibilities; 'the enemy of a true subjective fidelity is precisely the closed set [*ensemble*], the substance of the situation, the community' (Badiou, 1998/2001: 76).

Although I have started with an account of fidelity to the event and the emergence of 'Evil variants of the Good' (Barker, 2002: 140) in politics so far, this is not meant to serve as a model for the other spheres – love, science and art – except insofar as each function as homologous and as an illustration for the relation between fidelity and Evil in the other spheres. Let us turn to love. Fidelity to a loved one might be thought of as the creation of a certain kind of truth in which the relationship has the effect of reorganizing the field of choices that one makes. With respect to fidelity in love Badiou comments that 'under the effect of the loving encounter, if I want to be *really* faithful to it, I must completely rework my ordinary way of "living" my situation' (Badiou, 1998/2001: 42).

So, what might the simulacrum of love be? Perhaps, to take the example of the internal degeneration of the Russian Revolution and the anticipation of that degeneration in Kronstadt as an illustrative guide, we might think of the jealous attachment of a man to his partner and the expression of affection through violence against her as a 'terror' that represents itself as a continuation of love; but it actually appears as a transformation of the Good of the love relationship into Evil. The second form of appearance of Evil as betrayal is then easy enough to picture, as the weaving of lies in a relationship, perhaps to conceal the taking of another lover. It takes the form of betrayal not because of the empirical behaviour – it may not indeed be a betrayal if there had been agreement that it would be an 'open' relationship – but because it is contained within a fiction of fidelity to the Other. And the third form of Evil as totalization might be conceptualized in the frame of enveloping dependence in which the system of relations in a family unit, say, starts to become a coercive system in which there is no space for anything that differs from the dominant definition of what the relationship is. Every difference is condemned as the betrayal of love, and the patterns of accusation and recrimination would then function to hold the participants in place.

These forms of emergence of Evil have been characterized here as part of an internal degeneration of a love relationship, but if we are to move on to the reproduction of what passes for love in Western culture outside specific relationships, we might think of pornography as simulacrum of love, of the position of the deliberately isolated misanthrope or misogynist as betrayal, and the evangelical call for adherence to the call of a loving deity or religious leader in cults as betrayal of love. In these cases, of course, the separation from the sphere of politics is not actually so clear-cut, and the production of a position in love is also often a political position.

We have been describing the ways Evil emerges from a failure of the Good – in simulacrum, betrayal and totalization – so far in ways that seem rather remote from psychology. So, let us try and connect more explicitly with the problematic of ethics in psychology, and do that through a consideration of the remaining two spheres Badiou specifies, science and art.

Psychology is concerned not only with discipline but also with the anatomy of the mind, and this discipline of psychology works at the borders between science and art. Is it science or art, and how does it encounter ethics in its research practice?

At the risk of turning something that is already, perhaps, too much of a grid into a much too clear-cut framework for organizing how we think about research in psychology, I would suggest that one way of putting Badiou to work is as follows. We could think of the 'scientific' aspect of psychology, which has been dominant for the first short period of its existence after the experiments by Wilhelm Wundt in Leipzig (Danziger, 1990), as operating as a 'simulacrum' of science; that is, as the attempt to configure the human being as an object to be predicted and controlled. But the side of 'art' that some forms of qualitative research have claimed does not necessarily live up to that claim of being a progressive alternative. Of the studies in qualitative research that aim to respect the creativity of human beings, there are not many that are actually very creative or artistically enjoyable. The very academic production of knowledge in journal and textbook form leads qualitative research to operate as a simulacrum of art.

And we could also think of the discipline of psychology as science as a 'betrayal', for it does not even, for example, adhere to the reciprocal investigation of mental phenomena that Wundt was concerned with. The 'subject' of a supposedly scientific laboratory experiment is rendered into an object quite other to the investigator. Again, if we turn to qualitative research attempting to work on the art side of the science–art divide in psychology, we find much agonizing about the representation of the experience of others, but again and again an 'ethical' decision is made to betray those who have been interviewed or observed so that the material can be re-represented to an audience of psychologists.

And, as a third form of Evil in psychology, we could note ways in which the knowledge that the discipline produces is 'absolutized' so that descriptions from one limited group that behaves in a particular kind of setting controlled by the experimenter is then generalized and, through diagnostic and psychological treatment programmes, applied to make all subjects conform to that knowledge. Qualitative research has matched this normalization and pathologization of experience with its own romantic images of what the human being is like, how it develops and how it should be happy. It succumbs time after time to the temptation to tell us what 'universal' qualities of human experience are and to warn us against making those qualities into the substance of 'human rights' for everyone everywhere.

It is, perhaps, easy enough to complain about the present state of psychology and to condemn qualitative research as being the continuation, albeit as distorted mirror image, of the mainly quantitative practices it sometimes claims to oppose. But if we have identified forms of Evil in psychology as it appears in the spheres of science and art – its forms of simulacrum, betrayal and absolutization – how do we open up something new so that there could be fidelity to the event as a space for a different kind of subject and truth to emerge?

The questions raised about ethics by Lacan, and elaborated in relation to politics by Badiou, do not really amount to a new 'paradigm' for psychology, but they might lead us to a way of thinking about ethics in something approaching an 'anti-psychology', thinking close to it, and an alternative way of reflecting on what we usually assume the ethical benefits of qualitative research to be.

6 Psychoanalytic cyberspace, beyond psychology

This chapter makes an argument for Lacan's work as a specific form of representation grounded in contemporary internet communication media, in 'cyberspace' as a constellation of environments for contemporary subjectivity that includes virtual reality, chat-rooms and web-surfing. An underlying assumption in this chapter is that Freud's invention of the unconscious was of a piece with the development of particular forms of communication and what we like to think of as 'reality' under capitalism in the early twentieth century.

Psychoanalysis is a theory and practice of speech, and the 'talking cure' for the first century of psychoanalytic treatment required that the analyst be co-present to an analysand who was invited to follow the rule of free association. The necessary (and impossible) task of putting everything that comes to mind, however ridiculous or unpleasant, into words is embedded in a particular theory of representation and the insistence that talking to another person under transference is qualitatively different from writing things down.

So the argument here that Lacan's mutation of psychoanalysis as in keeping with contemporary 'virtual reality' has implications for some current debates about psychoanalytic practice. The process of sending queries to a psychoanalyst by email in order to solicit written interpretations would seem to be anathema to psychoanalysis, and now the increasing volume of traffic through cyberspace poses challenges to the very nature of the treatment. I was intrigued by FAQ12 to the Chair of the American Psychoanalytic

Association's Committee on Public Information which appeared on the 'Ask a Psychoanalyst' section of the APsaA website as follows: 'Can I do a psychoanalytical treatment through email? Do you know of any recognized psychoanalyst or organization that would?' The answer was forthright: 'I do not know of any psychoanalyst or psychoanalytic organization which sponsors or approves of on-line treatment.' Why?

This chapter examines the way cyberspace has emerged as a new anthropo-logical space, and how this space throws everyday commonsensical images of individual psychology into question. Psychology, a discipline that has aimed to undermine psychoanalytic practice on the grounds that a science of individual behaviour should be based on empirical 'evidence', has long drawn sustenance from computer-based forms of decision-making for mod-els of the mind as a perceptual–cognitive apparatus engaging in varieties of information-processing to negotiate reality. Now this orthodox psychol-ogy is at one moment unsettled by new virtual anthropological space where subjectivity seems to operate in quite different ways to those described in psychology textbooks, and at the next moment determined to colonize this space, to make the psychology of those at the interface with the com-puter compatible with behaviour occurring in new channels of electronic communication.

Psychoanalysis provides some quite different compass points for navigat-ing reality and fantasy in the 'real world' and so also in cyberspace, but this space also poses a question to psychoanalysis, as to whether it will really be willing to transform itself, in its theory and practice, in order to address the new forms of subjectivity that have been called forth in the world that has made cyberspace possible.

Anthropological space

Cyberspace provides a quite peculiar intersubjective space for its par-ticipants and gives rise to particular kinds of representation of human commu-nication for those who remain in the real world. The relationship between fantasies of cyberspace and fantasy in everyday life can be seen in the seepage of vocabulary from the virtual domain into everyday life (Barglow, 1994; Rushkoff, 1994). Examples include 'reality hacking' to describe engagement with the everyday world that draws upon the activities of software engineers and game-players, the 'matrix defence' employed to exculpate those who confused murder in reality with combat inside software-space, and the recent emergence of the term 'body spam' to describe unwanted touching in public places.

Cyberspace is a site for rehearsing assumptions about aspects of human nature in Western society, whether this nature is posited as the reverse – antithetical to what human relationships are supposed to be like – or absolute substrate when it serves to confirm the existence of the most destructive and excessive animal drives. Virtual reality environments proliferate in systems of electronically mediated communication in the bloated service sector that characterizes late capitalist society (Mandel, 1974). These environments produce new forms of subjectivity, versions of the self that break from orthodox modern conceptions (Gordo-López and Parker, 1999; Gray, 1995). If there is anything of importance for psychoanalysis in the ostensible transformation of culture into a 'postmodern condition' (Lyotard, 1979/1984), it lies in the new forms of subjectivity produced in new technologies, in particular in cyberspace (Featherstone and Burrows, 1995).

When people participate in the new electronic environments they configure themselves as different types of subject. Modes of interaction do not follow patterns found in either face-to-face or written communication, grammatical rules are different, and even forms of emotion have mutated through the use of 'emoticons' and particular forms of 'netiquette' (Shields, 1996). Those sitting at the computer terminals have not only entered a different environment, but the rules of discourse which govern that environment provide new conditions of possibility for action and experience. The study of different forms of life has put 'cross-cultural' psychology on the agenda again, but we need to approach this agenda with care (Gordo-López and Cleminson, 2004).

Cross-cultural psychology was much of the time concerned with comparing other cultures, 'primitives', with the advanced delights of modern civilization. This cross-cultural and anthropological work was still often mired in orientalist and racist notions of the 'other', though, and every ostensible break from 'our' way of being could be written off as being about different forms of underlying human 'nature'. At the same time, however, it could not help but re-present, in its descriptions of those 'others', something so different that it shook our conceptions about the nature of 'cognition', 'memory' and 'experience'. Traditional psychology, often quite unwittingly, used to produce radical critiques of the assumptions underlying the discipline about the 'nature' of 'human nature' when it studied 'other' cultures (Heelas and Lock, 1981).

Cyberspace functions in much the same way as the old anthropological spaces functioned in relation to Western civilization, as a space onto which to project fantasies about what is other to everyday life, a space in which people are supposed to do things very differently from us. The comparison between cyberspace as an anthropological space and the old faraway anthropological spaces is also relevant in terms of the ongoing process of colonization and control of what may be experienced as dangerous because it is other, because it is outside the frame of everyday commonsensical 'reality'. Now we are presented with an environment where different selves live, where they interface in peculiar ways, but where they are also *us*; the subjects we study in cyberspace, in a faraway place, inhabit the very same bodies that we interact with in the real world – life on-screen necessarily intersects with life off-screen (Gray, 1995).

The otherness of cyberspace is visible in the radicalization of the space. On the one side it is a space for economic fraud, in the spam letters that are reputed to account for one-third of the Nigerian gross domestic product, that emerge from a geographical space outside the West, the blank space on the map in which Africa figures as the least wired space, the past. On the other side it is space for identity formation, in the high-tech manga world of the 'otaku' in Japan, economically and electronically vibrant spaces which write the ground-rules for what this cyberspace will be like, the future (Saito, 2003).

Just as old anthropology was constituted as a series of representations that served to warrant the representations of self of the kind of subject suited to psychoanalytic inquiry and treatment in the West, so cyberspace now operates as a field of representation that appears to confirm necessary interconnections between the unconscious and sex (Rayban, 1995). As in old anthropology, cultural sites that are positioned as 'other' to civilization provide screens upon which is projected what is taken to be the deep underlying material of unconscious fantasy.

Psychology

Cyberspace provides a challenge to the technologies of surveillance and control that comprise the modern 'psy-complex' (the dense network of discourses and practices to do with the 'mind' and 'behaviour' that make up academic, popular and professional psychology). But we need to be clear what that challenge is, for the discipline of psychology is moving very fast to capture the 'psychology' of subjects in cyberspace (Wallace, 1999). Cyberspace does not provide a 'free space' in the way that some new-age feel-good writers seem to think. It is fluid, but structured. We are mobile, but constrained. Our 'psychology' in the 'real' world often appears to enjoy flexibility, mobility and choice (and we are invited to think that we enjoy these all the more so in so-called postmodern times), but is actually constituted by discourse and practices which limit our ability to think beyond this form of culture; likewise, our 'cyberspychology' in the 'electronic' world appears to offer an open horizon when that horizon is actually always already (under)written by corporate interests, institutions and power. This new 'cyberpsychology' needs to be located in relation to old psychology so we can see better what the stakes are for psychoanalytic alternatives (Gordo-López and Parker, 1999).

Modern psychology is constructed within particular fantasies of technology and space, culturally specific notions about the ways in which certain instruments can be put to work in delimited situations. The laboratory experiment, for example, is predicated upon the idea that certain variables can be identified and measured, and that a strictly bounded physical setting can contain, and be made to represent, certain psychological and social processes. Disciplinary technology as the means by which science will progress is, in the process, counterposed to the object of study, the human subject and its nature. A certain cluster of metaphors and practices holds modern psychology in place and at the centre of that cluster is a preoccupation with *sight*. There is a fantasy at the heart of modern psychology that every behaviour can be directly observed, laid open to the gaze of the investigator.

The discipline still operates, as does much knowledge in modern culture, within an epistemological and methodological framework that is governed by the language of vision (Jay, 1986). This 'modernity', with its wellsprings in the Western Enlightenment of the eighteenth century, traces and advertises narratives of personal meaning, progress, and science. While modern philosophy understood itself to be the 'mirror of nature' (Rorty, 1980), modern psychology developed the project of accurately mirroring and measuring behaviour, and finding the distorted reflections or hallucinations of mental states there.

The corpus of knowledge that psychologists have accumulated through careful observation and analysis of data is not just an illusion, however, and the image of the person as a separate and selfcontained individual, an image that psychology reproduces, corresponds much of the time to the lived reality of its subjects. The modern discipline tabulates and regulates a population of already modern subjects schooled to anticipate and understand themselves in psychological texts. As part of an ostensibly 'modern' age, psychology faithfully reflects and supports the dominant culture (Ingleby, 1985; Rose, 1985). However, there has, to some extent, always been a problem, expressed in the resistance of subjects to racist classifications of mental abilities or to attempts to root competitiveness and the capitalist spirit in the depths of unchanging and unchangeable human nature.

We can understand the role of this problem in psychological knowledge by saying that the common sense that psychology picked up and recycled was modern but always *contradictory*. A measure of interpretation was necessary to ensure that the ruling ideas were the ideas that would be located in the heads of those that were ruled. And the problem, that there are contradictory and fragmentary actual psychologies that people live in different spaces, is now intensified by changes in technology that open up *new* spaces and new subjectivities, subjectivities that modern psychology finds it all the more difficult to comprehend. These changes in technology have, as their most important characteristic, the ability to construct new 'virtual realities' in which the human subject feels that they have left their body to move around in a completely different space. The problem of contradiction and resistance to psychological knowledge is expressed now at its extreme in the claim that the modern corpus of knowledge is dying away, and that new 'postmodern' psychologies are taking flight from it, and taking flight from the body (Gergen, 1991; Kvale, 1992).

The first defining account of the supposed shift from 'modern' to 'postmodern' society was first written, it should be remembered, as 'a report on knowledge' (Lyotard, 1979/1984), as a fairly systematic survey of the political and commercial opportunities offered by information technology. The phrase 'postmodern', which had already been popularized in architectural theory, caught the imagination of some artists and academics whose lifestyles had been boosted to the status of minor celebrities and, in the process, been disconnected from the mass of the working class and Third World poor. It also warranted a flight from politics among activists and writers in their forties and fifties who were burnt out and disappointed with the ebb of radical movements in the industrialized world. Much of postmodern mythology is bewitched with the power of language understood as no more than a string of images, and the disintegration of any 'real' outside such images. Advertising and media constructions – symbiotic growths upon this rapidly mutating economic structure – represent this world to the rest of the world as an incomprehensible kaleidoscopic widescreen in which the real and the artificial are confused to the point where intervention seems pointless and impossible (Baudrillard, 1973/1975).

The impossibility of action is interwoven with an ethic of intensity of experience; a narcissistic hedonism that fills the lack that consumerism without frontiers has constituted, a narcissism that can be interpreted using psychoanalytic categories as a complement to the analysis of 'postmodernism' (Lasch, 1978). Postmodern consumer culture, in this respect, offers some consolation to a public that is often too bewildered to participate in politics, and to erstwhile political activists who despair of changing it. The explosion and power of media surfaces that operate in this way could be written off as being but further twists in the ideological mystification that has accompanied capitalism from its earliest days.

There is something of a paradox, then, in the emergence of 'postmodernism' inside the discipline of psychology as a radical slogan to gather together critiques of laboratory experimentation and other dehumanizing practices in the discipline (Parker, 1998). To say that it is a paradox does not mean, of course, to say that it is wholly retrograde, and 'postmodern psychology' has become, in some places, a legitimating umbrella term for a variety of innovative approaches ranging from grounded theory to discourse analysis (Parker, 2002).

The break from modern psychology's mission of steadily accumulating scientific facts about the human subject in the name of postmodernism is still progressive then, for human psychology is indeed always too contradictory and transient, too social and selftransformative to be captured in the way the discipline would have liked. This is where there is an opening for psychoanalysis inside and against psychology, but this needs to be a form of psychoanalysis that is resolutely 'anti-psychological' (Parker, 2003). It needs to go beyond old psychology and beyond the perspectives of the selfstyled postmoderns in psychology who try to deny that there are any relatively enduring restrictions to social action, to deny that we could understand such restrictions with reference to an economic system that can be known, and so can then be transformed. We need to keep focused on the problem that contradictory resistant human agency poses for psychology, and upon psychology as part of the problem. The discipline of psychology wedded to science and to technologies of factory management emphasized containment and order, and it was left to another discipline, another critical modern theoretical system, psychoanalysis, to focus on the other side of the tension, transformation and self-knowledge.

Psychoanalysis

Anthropological space operated as a condition of possibility for the development of psychoanalysis, for the forms of otherness that could be configured as lying outside the ego of the civilized were screens on which to play out the motifs of uncivilized, barbaric and untamed human nature, arenas in which rational scientific debate could take place to appraise and evaluate speculations about the reality of historically sedimented and accumulating human experience as consciousness became differentiated from the unconscious (Freud, 1913 [1912–1913], 1930). The focus on consciousness invites a reduction back to psychology, while a focus on the unconscious leads to genuine psychoanalytic alternatives equipped to conceptualize the human subject in virtual space.

Psychoanalysis should be understood in its broadest sense here to encompass views of reality as being underpinned and undercut by dynamic unconscious processes. The unconscious erupts in dreams, jokes and slips and is powered by sexual desire. This desire is conceptualized in different ways by postFreudian writers, and it enters the vocabulary of culture through talk about infantile sexuality, need for relatedness, or the desire for recognition. It is that last, Lacanian, sense of disruptive unconscious desire that is at issue here and it is very different from the non-conscious mental processing conceptualized by psychologists (Malone and Friedlander, 2000). Psychoanalysis has operated over the last century as psychology's rival and twin, and its presence in popular theories of the self in Western culture has made it a key player in any adequate account of culturalmental mutations (Parker, 1997b). We can use versions of psychoanalytic theory to understand some of the emerging fantasies about ostensibly 'postmodern' subjectivity in cyberspace, but we will also need to attend to the way that psychoanalytic theory itself is reproduced in those fantasies.

Lacanian psychoanalysis does not treat as empirical definable substance any of the paraphernalia that characterize accounts of psychoanalysis in psychology textbooks. From the beginning of his work, way before the famous turn to language and structuralist theoretical resources, there was a refusal to explain Oedipal relationships by way of reference to biological evolution (Lacan, 1938). Lacan points out that his approach 'implies no recognition of any substance on which it claims to operate, even that of sexuality' (Lacan, 1964/1973: 266). The 'unconscious', for example, is a quality of speech, and Lacanian psychoanalysts track the moment-by-moment reconstruction of consciousness and what becomes structurally unavailable to it.

This opens up Lacanian psychoanalysis to a historically grounded account, and to 'techno-sexual' analyses of the relationship between technology and subjectivity (Gordo-López and Cleminson, 2004). Cyberspace raises questions about the relationship between reality and dreaming, between the ostensibly rock-solid perception and cognition of everyday life on the one hand, and the fantasy-suffused productions that appear when the censorship of the ego is relaxed. Cyberspace stands in relation to 'reality' as a kind of dream-space that Lacanian psychoanalysis is eminently suited to comprehend.

One can imagine cyberspace as operating like a dream, and this analogy is useful as a way in to the analysis, because it enables us to treat cyberspace as a kind of text that can be interpreted using psychoanalysis. Here we need to avoid psychologized versions of psychoanalysis as a way of thinking about the retrieval of 'latent content' as the real meaning of the dream obscured by the 'manifest content' as something we have to pull aside. The question is not what has been obscured, but how it is being covered over (Freud, 1900/1999). We are not trying to dig up things from under the surface, but to show how the surface of the text itself constitutes certain objects, subjects and relationships between them, and how it also at the same moment covers them over. That is, the different forms of representation and mechanisms of defence produce the objects they so painstakingly shield themselves against. The predicament of the neurotic, of course, is that the work they do to defend themselves against threat is precisely their problem; it causes them more pain than the things that they try to avoid thinking about, and in not thinking about them these things assume overwhelming magnitude in their thoughts.

When we treat cyberspace as like a dream text the relationship between the text as a fantasmatic frame on the one hand and 'reality' on the other is thrown into question. It is precisely that questioning of the boundaries between on-screen representation and everyday reality that leads some writers to claim that contemporary reality is effectively cinematic (Baudrillard, 1973/1975). What we call reality is suffused with fantasy, and all the more so for Lacanian psychoanalysis than Anglo-American ego-psychology, for which there is a 'conflict-free sphere' of the ego that apprehends reality (Hartmann, 1939/1958). However, this does not mean that 'life is a dream' as far as Lacan is concerned. It is important that we be able to tell the difference between a dream and waking life. The way we tell the difference between a dream and waking life is also relevant to the way we tell the difference between cyberspace and life off-screen. Two Lacanian concepts are relevant here: the gaze and the real.

Lacan draws attention to the role of the gaze in the fantasmatic frame of the subject in his brief discussion of the Chinese philosopher Choang-tsu's dream of being a butterfly, and the thought when he awakes that he, Choang-tsu, may now be a butterfly dreaming of being a Chinese philosopher. For Lacan, it is a key defining characteristic of waking consciousness that we are always in the gaze of the Other, present to them as a function of being a human subject. It is this very difference from himself, when he is awake, that now makes it possible for Choang-tsu to puzzle about what he was when he was the butterfly. To be a butterfly is, Lacan says, but 'one of the roots of his identity', an identity he is glued to in the dream. He is glued to it to such a degree that there is no other in whose gaze he can take a distance and wonder whether he may be merely the dream of a Chinese philosopher: Lacan points out that 'in the dream, he [Choang-tsu] is a butterfly for nobody. It is when he is awake that he is Choang-tsu for others, and is caught in their butterfly net' (Lacan, 1964/1973: 76).

The second key concept Lacan employs is the 'real'. The real is important conceptually to make sense of how it is that someone is woken from a dream. Dreams for Freud (1900/1999) are the 'guardians of sleep', but they sometimes fail to do the work of representing traumatic material and coding it in such a way that they can simultaneously disguise and express that material. Lacan's discussion of the father – woken when he dreams of his dead son saying to him, 'Father, can't you see I'm burning?' to find that there is indeed a fire in the next room which has caught onto the bed with his son's body in it (Freud, 1900/1999) – illustrates how it is that the 'split in the subject appears'. For Lacan, it is at the moment when the real hits the dream as an impossible-to-represent kernel – resistant to comfortable recoding within the fantasmatic frame that constitutes the manifest content of the dream – that the dreamer awakes. They awake from the dream so that they can carry on dreaming with their eyes open. There is, however, a difference between dreaming with your eyes open and being at the mercy of a dream inside the dream. It is precisely that difference that is inscribed in dreaming with your eyes open, inscribed as a 'split in the subject'. The split in the subject upon awakening is between 'a return to the real' on the one hand and, on the other hand, Lacan says, 'consciousness re-weaving itself, which knows it is living through all this as through a nightmare, but which, all the same, keeps a grip on itself' (Lacan, 1964/1973: 70).

It is evident here that Lacan is not at all a pop 'postmodernist' celebrating fragmentation and unreason. Psychoanalysis is part of the Enlightenment project of reasoning self-inquiry carried out in the presence of another. Life is not a dream for Lacan, even if, like a dream, our life in the symbolic order can shield us against the real, and when we are in 'reality', in the symbolic, we live in the gaze of the Other as a guarantee of our conscious awareness of what the difference is between what it is to dream and what it is to be awake, what it is to be a man and what it is to be a woman in this reality (Adams, 1996).

To be immersed in cyberspace is to be thrown into a similar set of paradoxes. But when entering cyberspace we are within a kind of dreamscape that still operates as if it were reality. To be caught in the gaze of cyberspace is to be subject to forms of identification and interpellation that only operate insofar as we know that we are subjects surfing cyberspace; to be hit by the real in cyberspace – at moments of shock that break the illusion of self-sufficient representation structured by the software – is but a moment of disturbance that we know will be 'sutured' such that the fantasmatic frame will be repaired. Cyberspace is boundaried by the process of logging in and out such that we expect that the narrative at one part of the communication broken at one moment will be restored at the next.

This is not to say that cyberspace as such is really *only* a dream-space, or that clicking through websites and typing messages in chat-rooms necessarily entails the hallucinatory production of a form of subjectivity closer to the unconscious. Fluid and fragmented subjectivity in front of the computer may be more prevalent than when we are in the real world, but the key issue here is how that cyberspace is constituted as other to the real world, constituted as if it were like a dream in relation to what still feels like brute reality.

Locating psychoanalysis

Cyberspace is a function of the imaginative framing, speculation and taming of a world beyond everyday reality. Psychoanalysis is woven into the experience of cyberspace, for it is psychoanalysis that provides the coordinates for making sense of this new space as something that lies outside rational civilized human relationships. There certainly could be computers, electronic communication and fields of visual representation distributed between servers without psychoanalysis, but there could not be 'cyberspace' as such.

Psychoanalysis can be used to interpret cyberspace then, but this task is too easy, only the first step. The symbolic forms and imaginative productions that circulate around cyberspace are already constituted by psychoanalytic categories, and the individual subjects who encounter virtual reality already posit that virtual reality as something equivalent to the preconscious at best and the unconscious at worst, bedevilled by the venal fantasy productions of others. Psychoanalytic interpretation is not one of the solutions; it is, rather, part of the very phenomenon that it pretends to explain.

Studies of the suffusion of psychoanalysis through popular culture in France, and detailed studies of the social representations of psychoanalysis in that culture are paralleled by sociological work in America in the 1960s and in Britain in the 1970s which have each traced the 'cultural affinity' of contemporary culture with psychoanalytic categories (Berger, 1965; Bocock, 1976; Moscovici, 1976/2008). These accounts are then compatible with a social constructionist view of the cultural transmission of psychological knowledge from the social through to the interior of the subject (Parker, 1997b).

Psychoanalysis as a theoretical system and clinical practice had to be pieced together for us so that it made sense and felt as if it must be right. There are a range of sensations we take for granted for psychoanalysis to become true for us. Rather than treat psychoanalysis simply as a key to unlock the secrets of the subject, then, we need to explore how psychoanalysis has been fashioned as part of a particular system of self-talk and self-reference. Psychoanalytic theory should be treated here as a powerful framework because psychoanalytic knowledge helps structure culture. Psychoanalysis should look to the collective cultural resources that structure our sense of our selves and those aspects of our lives that lie outside conscious awareness.

The turn away from a scientific and materialist account of the mind, to the realms of art and mythology as an alternative foundation for psychoanalysis free of any pretence to be any kind of science, goes back at least as far as Jung. Freud's attempts to delve into anthropology and to propose Lamarckian models of the acquisition of historical memories were driven, in part, by an attempt to provide a more properly materialist account. It is possible to take up the argument that there is some form of 'collective unconscious', but to reconfigure it as a historically constituted symbolic resource rather than something lying in a mysterious spiritual realm.

Collective resources are not floating beneath the personal unconscious of each of us, but *within* an 'unconscious' textual realm, the realm of discourse, and now within the realm of cyberspace as a particular form of writing initially constituted by machine-code. The history of writing shows that 'like words and text, memory is a child of the alphabet' (Illich and Sanders, 1988: 15), and now the particular form of writing that underpins virtual reality produces forms of subject defined by the parameters of symbolic logic (Bolter, 1986: 71). A multiplicity of tacit understandings, unacknowledged assumptions and unintended consequences frame our lives as we encounter and manage virtual social practices.

There are some similarities between this position and that advocated by Vološinov (1927/1973), which, although critical of Freudian discourse, elaborated many psychoanalytic tenets into a linguistically based system. Collective textual phenomena would then be closer to a transpersonal level of meaning that Foulkes (1986), writing in the group analysis tradition, refers to, or to the unconscious as an aspect of the symbolic order that Lacan describes. The unconscious is then itself treated, as Lacan (1964/1973) argued it should be, as 'the discourse of the Other' (with the 'Other' here being the symbolic system that holds culture in place and determines the location of each individual speaking subject). This notion of the unconscious also attends to the insistent perpetual inconsistency of sense in language. It allows us to develop an account of tacit assumptions, unacknowledged conditions and unintended consequences, *and* to account for the contradictory ways in which these mesh with structures of power that are relayed through different forms of virtual reality.

Cyberspace is constituted as a collective space, something closer to the transpersonal than to the collective phenomena described by Freud (1921) as the basis of an account of identification and individuation (Lacan, 1961–1962), something that stands in ambivalent relation to the individualized subjects who enter it and imagine that they will lose themselves. The position at each side of the equation – the individual at the interface and the intersubjective field of communication they enter – is a function of the technology that demands that each subject participates one by one and that every subject is governed by rules written to stipulate the activities of a generalized subject.

There are many different psychoanalytic resources with competing vocabularies, and so we need to acknowledge that there is no one correct interpretation, nor one correct psychoanalytic system for the wording of an interpretation. It is possible that the cultural location of psychoanalytic systems makes each of those systems specifically applicable to their cultures. It is the nature of the unconscious (the unconscious produced for us in culture now) to be riven by contradictory significations, and the nature of contemporary consciousness is to tolerate these contradictions, and to smooth them over. Psychoanalysis is a rational therapeutic enterprise, a theoretical framework in and against the human sciences which is designed to notice contradiction. We struggle, then, over the tension between different contradictory understandings. Each version of psychoanalysis has an appeal within specific cultural arenas, and it would be a mistake to propose one version as applicable to all.

However, when translated across the geographical, linguistic and political boundaries that mark off sectors of Western culture, each version of psychoanalysis hooks something in us. As Lacan points out in Seminar IX, 'every time there is progress in writing it is in so far as a population tried to symbolise its own language, its own phonematic articulation with the help of a writing material borrowed from another population' (Lacan, 1961–1962, 20 December 1961: 13). It is through the process of *translation* that a different intersubjective domain constituted by a different form of writing comes into being.

There is a second aspect of this contradictoriness of psychoanalysis in culture that is necessary to grasp, which is that there are many forms of psychoanalysis working simultaneously. Different individuals may have recourse to different forms of psychoanalytic argument on different occasions to understand themselves. Even resistance or the attempt to repudiate a certain form of psychoanalysis may be voiced from within a discursive framework that is structured by other different competing psychoanalytic suppositions. Cyberspace is a contradictory fantasy space that is interwoven with everyday 'reality' in complex relations of mistranslation and incomprehension. The necessary real of contradiction is no more evident in forms of 'gender' and in the anchoring of gender to 'sex'.

Psychoanalysis is implicated in every form of creative activity under capitalism, but we need to include in our analyses the way psychoanalytic modes of subjectivity were constituted by this activity (Parker, 1997b). Forms of novel-writing that were developed coterminous with the emergence of early psychoanalytic notions, for example, were themselves then inhabited by psychoanalytic notions of repression, unconscious desire and a life-course which would see the unravelling of a trajectory that had been laid down early inevitably waiting to come to fruition or grief. The development of the novel necessarily reconfigured forms of gender relations, and this form of writing constitutes the notion of sexual difference as a material base upon which the lived architecture of sensibility and coping is built as appropriate to each sex and in relation to the 'other' sex. The individual-ized life-narrative that the novel renders visible, and which then operates as one of the templates for the individual life experience of the reader of the novel, enables the elaboration of specific gendered sensibilities that can be configured as 'masculine' obsession or 'feminine' hysteria, and it is from these representational practices that psychoanalysis arises (Parker, 1997b). The novel itself then fractures into different forms of science fiction that constitute different forms of subject (Bukatman, 1993).

Cyberspace is gendered space, manifest in the images of emotionally incompetent young men taking refuge in the computer, in the constitution of masculine categories of subject who inhabit the virtual realm and quasi-virtual spaces, the consumers of game-ware. The gendered quality of cyber-space is also apparent in the attempt to reclaim the space for women in forms of 'cyberfeminism', in the refusal to allow this space to be dominated by men (Marsden, 1999) – also in the position of women as the super-exploited workforce typing in real-world texts into electronic format to provide the material basis for virtual reality.

Cyberspace is, at the same time, the fantasy of sexed space as the space of sex, and as a fantasy space that is structured by psychoanalytic catego-ries it would be surprising if it were not also the site of sex. It is the site of uninhibited sexual representation, imagined to be closer to the unconscious, flowing from site to site, emanating from 'off-shore' locations that are out-side the rule of law. It is, it is feared in the fantasies about this fantasy space, a number of quick clicks to pornography in cyberspace, and only a question of time before everyday sexuality is perverted by the seductions of breaking taboos relating to women and children, to animals and incest. Cyberspace as sexed space is, however, actually the site of the dirtiest secrets of con-temporary capitalism, the secret that it is economic exploitation that makes this space possible and that money must be sucked from the consumers to keep websites in business. In this way sex operates as the fantasy screen to conceal something even more unthinkable, the real of capitalist society. Beneath the proliferation of the 'sex-sites', the most immediate and sali-ent formations of the internet, are the incitements to spend money, whether through shopping, online gambling or credit card fraud. The real conditions of possibility for the development of new virtual spaces are tied to the devel-opment of the political-economic space of contemporary 'late' capitalism (Mandel, 1974).

Space for psychoanalysis now

The destruction of old anthropological spaces has also meant the destruction of sites upon which traditional psychoanalytic categories could be exercised.

The apparatus of old psychoanalysis – the role of the incest taboo as universal, the operation of paternity beyond the actual presence of the father, the insistence of infantile sexual and aggressive impulses as closer to nature – has been dismantled as the old research programmes for understanding 'primitive' forms of human relation have been closed down. Cyberspace gives psychoanalysis a new lease of life, but this space requires something new from psychoanalysis, and this is why forms of psychoanalysis oriented to the virtual, to the production of categories in the field of representation, have thrived. Forms of psychoanalysis that are built about the desubstantialization of categories of the object, those that focus on the circulation of the drives around virtual points, are best suited to this domain. These forms of psychoanalysis, however, still have to undergo theoretical transformation to tackle the production of new forms of subjectivity and new symptoms in changing landscapes of social relations (Britton, 2004).

At the same time, the looming threat of cyberspace, the suspicion that what is most real about human nature might be swept away in virtual relationships, also incites other pre-psychoanalytic and anti-psychoanalytic forms of psychology that pretend to fix universal and timeless human experience. The virtual world inspires a return to the categories of instinct and embodiment, a return to what refuses the immaterial and intangible world of the codes. This is a regression to the body that is provoked by a fantasy about where the destruction of the body might lead.

The endeavour to show that subjectivity is constructed, whether in cyberspace or in any other sector of late capitalist society, has to be combined with a deconstruction of subjectivity, the point at which our interpretations become mutative interpretations, where we take responsibility as agents in the world, not only interpreting but also changing it.

References

Adams, P. (1996) *The Emptiness of the Image: Psychoanalysis and Sexual Differences*. London: Routledge.

Althusser, L. (1971) *Lenin and Philosophy and Other Essays*. London: New Left Books.

Badiou, A. (1998/2001) *Ethics: An Essay on the Understanding of Evil*. London: Verso.

Badiou, A. (1998) 'Politics and philosophy: An interview with Alain Badiou', in A. Badiou (1998/2001) *Ethics: An Essay on the Understanding of Evil*. London: Verso.

Barglow, R. (1994) *The Crisis of the Self in the Age of Information: Computers, Dolphins and Dreams*. London: Routledge.

Barker, J. (2002) *Alain Badiou: A Critical Introduction*. London: Pluto Press.

Baudrillard, J. (1973/1975) *The Mirror of Production*. St. Louis: Telos Press.

Bennett, T. (1979) *Formalism and Marxism*. London: Methuen.

Bensaïd, D. (2002) *Marx for Our Times: Adventures and Misadventures of a Critique*. London: Verso.

Benvenuto, B. and Kennedy, R. (1986) *The Works of Jacques Lacan: An Introduction*. London: Free Association Books.

Berger, P.L. (1965) 'Towards a sociological understanding of psychoanalysis', *Social Research*, 32, 26–41.

Billig, M. (1976) *Social Psychology and Intergroup Relations*. London: Academic Press.

Billig, M. (1999) *Freudian Repression: Conversation Creating the Unconscious*. Cambridge: Cambridge University Press.

Blackman, D.E. (1980) 'Images of man in contemporary behaviourism', in A.J. Chapman and D.M. Jones (eds) *Models of Man*. Leicester: British Psychological Society.

Bocock, R. (1976) *Freud and Modern Society*. London: Van Nostrand Reinhold.

Bolter, J.D. (1986) *Turing's Man: Western Culture in the Computer Age*. Harmondsworth: Penguin.

Bottomore, T. (ed.) (1991) *A Dictionary of Marxist Thought* (second edition). Oxford: Blackwell.

Bracher, M. (1993) *Lacan, Discourse and Social Change: A Psychoanalytic Cultural Criticism*. Ithaca/London: Cornell University Press.

Britton, H. (2004) 'Contemporary symptoms and the challenge for psychoanalysis', *Journal for Lacanian Studies*, 2(1), 54–62.

Bukatman, S. (1993) *Terminal Identity: The Virtual Subject in Post-Modern Science Fiction*. Durham, NC: Duke University Press.

Burgoyne, B. (1997) 'Interpretation', in B. Burgoyne and M. Sullivan (eds) *The Klein–Lacan Dialogues*. London: Rebus Press.

Burgoyne, B. and Sullivan, M. (eds) (1997) *The Klein–Lacan Dialogues*. London: Rebus Press.

Burman, E. (1998) *Deconstructing Feminist Psychology*. London/Thousand Oaks, CA: Sage.

Burman, E. (2008a) *Deconstructing Developmental Psychology* (second edition). Abingdon/New York: Routledge.

Burman, E. (2008b) *Developments: Child, Image, Nation*. Abingdon and New York: Routledge.

Burman, E., Aitken, G., Alldred, P., Allwood, R., Billington, T., Goldberg, B., Gordo-López, A., Heenan, C., Marks, D. and Warner, S. (1996) *Psychology Discourse Practice: From Regulation to Resistance*. London: Taylor and Francis.

Burr, V. (2003) *Social Constructionism* (second edition). London/New York: Routledge.

Butler, J. (1990) *Gender Trouble: Feminism and the Subversion of Identity*. London/New York: Routledge.

Butler, J. (2000) *Antigone's Claim: Kinship Between Life and Death*. New York: Columbia University Press.

Catania, A.C. (1973) 'The concept of the operant in the analysis of behavior', *Behaviourism*, 1(2), 103–116.

Chandra, S. (1976) 'Repression, dreaming and primary process thinking: Skinnerism formulations of some Freudian facts', *Behaviourism*, 4(1), 53–75.

Clifford, J. and Marcus, G. (eds) (1986) *Writing Culture: The Poetics and Politics of Ethnography*. Berkeley, CA: University of California Press.

Curt, B. (1994) *Textuality and Tectonics: Troubling Social and Psychological Science*. Buckingham: Open University Press.

Cushman, P. (1991) 'Ideology obscured: Political uses of the self in Daniel Stern's infant', in I. Parker (ed.) (2011) *Critical Psychology: Critical Concepts in Psychology, Vol. 3, Psychologisation and Psychological Culture*. London and New York: Routledge.

Danziger, K. (1990) *Constructing the Subject: Historical Origins of Psychological Research*. Cambridge: Cambridge University Press.

Day, W. (1977) 'On the behavioral analysis of self-deception and self-development', in T. Mischel (ed.) *The Self: Psychological and Philosophical Issues*. Oxford: Blackwell.

Day, W. (1983) 'On the difference between radical and methodological behaviourism', *Behaviourism*, 11(1), 89–102.

Derrida, J. (1981) *Positions*. London: Athlone Press.

110   References

Descombes, V. (1980) *Modern French Philosophy*. Cambridge: Cambridge University Press.

De Vos, J. (2012) *Psychologisation in Times of Globalisation*. Abingdon and New York: Routledge.

Dreyfus, H.L. (1967) 'Why computers must have bodies in order to be intelligent', *Review of Metaphysics*, 21, 13–32.

Dunker, C. (2008) 'Psychology and psychoanalysis in Brazil: From cultural syncretism to the collapse of liberal individualism', *Theory & Psychology*, 18(2), 223–236.

Dunker, C. (2010) *The Structure and Constitution of the Psychoanalytic Clinic: Negativity and Conflict in Contemporary Practice*. London: Karnac.

Eagleton, T. (1983) *Literary Theory: An Introduction*. Oxford: Blackwell.

Edwards, D. (1992) *Discourse and Cognition*. London: Sage.

Ellis, C. and Bochner, A.P. (2000) 'Autoethnography, personal narrative, reflexivity', in N.K. Denzin and Y.S. Lincoln (eds) *Handbook of Qualitative Research* (second edition). Thousand Oaks, CA: Sage.

Evans, D. (1996) *An Introductory Dictionary of Lacanian Psychoanalysis*. London: Routledge.

Featherstone, M. and Burrows, R. (eds) (1995) *Cyberspace/Cyberbodies/Cyberpunk: Cultures of Embodiment*. London: Sage.

Feldstein, R., Fink, B. and Jaanus, M. (eds) (1995) *Reading Seminar XI: Lacan's Four Fundamental Concepts of Psychoanalysis*. New York: SUNY Press.

Feldstein, R., Fink, B. and Jaanus, M. (eds) (1996) *Reading Seminars I and II: Lacan's Return to Freud*. New York: SUNY Press.

Feyerabend, P. (1978) *Against Method: Outline of an Anarchistic Theory of Knowledge*. London: Verso.

Filmer, P. (1972) 'On Harold Garfinkel's ethnomethodology', in P. Filmer, M. Phillipson, D. Silverman and D. Walsh (eds) *New Directions in Sociological Theory*. London: Collier/Macmillan.

Fink, B. (1995) *The Lacanian Subject: Between Language and Jouissance*. Princeton, NJ: Princeton University Press.

Fink, B. (1997) *A Clinical Introduction to Lacanian Psychoanalysis: Theory and Technique*. Cambridge, MA: Harvard University Press.

Fodor, J. (1983) *The Modularity of Mind*. Cambridge, MA: MIT Press.

Foucault, M. (1966/1970) *The Order of Things*. London: Tavistock.

Foucault, M. (1969/1972) *The Archaeology of Knowledge*. London: Tavistock.

Foucault, M. (1975/1979) *Discipline and Punish: The Birth of the Prison*. Harmondsworth: Penguin.

Foucault, M. (1976/1981) *The History of Sexuality, Vol. I: An Introduction*. Harmondsworth: Pelican.

Foucault, M. (1980) *Power/Knowledge Selected Interviews and Other Writings 1972–1977*. Hassocks, Sussex: Harvester Press.

Foulkes, S.H. (1986) *Group-Analytic Therapy: Methods and Principles*. London: Karnac.

Fox, D. and Prilleltensky, I. (eds) (1997) *Critical Psychology: An Introduction*. London: Sage.

Freud, S. (1900/1999) *The Interpretation of Dreams* (translated by J. Crick). Oxford: Oxford University Press.

Freud, S. (1913 [1912–1913]) 'Totem and taboo', in S. Freud (1966–1974) *The Standard Edition of the Complete Psychological Works of Sigmund Freud, Vol. XIII* (translated by J. Strachey). London: Vintage, Hogarth Press and Institute of Psycho-Analysis.

Freud, S. (1915) 'Observations on transference-love (further recommendations on the technique of psycho-analysis III)', in S. Freud (1966–1974) *The Standard Edition of the Complete Psychological Works of Sigmund Freud, Vol. XII* (translated by J. Strachey). London: Vintage, Hogarth Press and Institute of Psycho-Analysis.

Freud, S. (1920) 'Beyond the pleasure principle', in S. Freud (1966–1974) *The Standard Edition of the Complete Psychological Works of Sigmund Freud, Vol. XVIII* (translated by J. Strachey). London: Vintage, Hogarth Press and Institute of Psycho-Analysis.

Freud, S. (1921) 'Group psychology and the analysis of the ego', in S. Freud (1966–1974) *The Standard Edition of the Complete Psychological Works of Sigmund Freud, Vol. XVIII* (translated by J. Strachey). London: Vintage, Hogarth Press and Institute of Psycho-Analysis.

Freud, S. (1927) 'Fetishism', in S. Freud (1966–1974) *The Standard Edition of the Complete Psychological Works of Sigmund Freud, Vol. XX!* (translated by J. Strachey). London: Vintage, Hogarth Press and Institute of Psycho-Analysis.

Freud, S. (1930) 'Civilization and its discontents', in S. Freud (1966–1974) *The Standard Edition of the Complete Psychological Works of Sigmund Freud, Vol. XXI* (translated by J. Strachey). London: Vintage, Hogarth Press and Institute of Psycho-Analysis.

Freud, S. (1933) 'New introductory lectures on psychoanalysis', in S. Freud (1966–1974) *The Standard Edition of the Complete Psychological Works of Sigmund Freud, Vol. XXII* (translated by J. Strachey). London: Vintage, The Hogarth Press and the Institute of Psycho-Analysis.

Freud, S. (1953–1974) *The Standard Edition of the Complete Psychological Works of Sigmund Freud* (24 vols) (translated by J. Strachey). London: Vintage, The Hogarth Press and the Institute of Psycho-Analysis.

Frosh, S. (1989) *Psychoanalysis and Psychology: Minding the Gap*. London: Macmillan.

Frosh, S. (1997) *For and Against Psychoanalysis*. London: Routledge.

Gergen, K.J. (1999) *An Invitation to Social Construction*. London: Sage.

Gergen, K.J. (1985) 'The social constructionist movement in modern psychology', *American Psychologist*, 40(3), 266–275.

Gergen, K.J. (1991) *The Saturated Self: Dilemmas of Identity in Contemporary Life*. New York: Basic Books.

Gordo-López, A.J. (2000) 'On the psychologization of critical psychology', *Annual Review of Critical Psychology*, 2, 55–71.

Gordo-López, A.J. and Cleminson, M.R. (2004) *Techno-Sexual Landscapes: Changing Relations between Technology and Sexuality*. London: Free Association Books.

Gordo-López, A.J. and Parker, I. (eds) (1999) *Cyberpsychology*. London: Macmillan.

Gray, C.H. (ed.) (1995) *The Cyborg Handbook*. New York: Routledge.

Greenberg, J. and Mitchell, S. (1983) *Object Relations in Psychoanalytic Theory*. Cambridge, MA: Harvard University Press.

Habermas, J. (1971) *Knowledge and Human Interests*. London: Heinemann.

Hacking, I. (1996) 'Memory sciences, memory politics', in P. Antze and M. Lambek (eds) *Tense Past: Cultural Essays in Trauma and Memory*. London/New York: Routledge.

Hallward, (2001) 'Translator's Introduction', in A. Badiou, *Ethics: An Essay on the Understanding of Evil*. London: Verso.

Harré, R. (1979) *Social Being: A Theory for Social Psychology*. Oxford: Blackwell.

Harré, R. (ed.) (1986) *The Social Construction of Emotions*. Oxford: Blackwell.

Harre, R. and Mühlhäusler, P. (1990) *Pronouns and People*. Oxford: Blackwell.

Harré, R. and Secord, P.F. (1972) *The Explanation of Social Behaviour*. Oxford: Blackwell.

Hartmann, H. (1939/1958) *Ego Psychology and the Problem of Adaptation*. New York: International Universities Press.

Heelas, P. and Lock, A. (eds) (1981) *Indigenous Psychologies: The Anthropology of the Self*. London: Academic Press.

Hegel, G.W.F. (1807/1977) *Philosophy of Spirit* (translated by A.V. Miller). Oxford: Oxford University Press.

Heidegger, M. (1928/1962) *Being and Time*. Oxford: Blackwell.

Henriques, J., Hollway, W., Urwin, C., Venn, C. and Walkerdine, V. (1984/1998) *Changing the Subject: Psychology, Social Regulation and Subjectivity*. London/ New York: Routledge.

Hollway, W. (1989) *Subjectivity and Method in Psychology: Gender, Meaning and Science*. London: Sage.

Hook, D. (2007) *Foucault, Psychology and the Analytics of Power*. London: Palgrave.

Illich, I. and Sanders, B. (1988) *ABC: The Alphabetization of the Popular Mind*. Harmondsworth: Pelican.

Ingleby, D. (1985) 'Professionals as socializers: The "psy complex"', in I. Parker (ed.) (2011) *Critical Psychology: Critical Concepts in Psychology, Vol. 1, Dominant Models of Psychology and Their Limits* (pp. 279–307). London and New York: Routledge.

Jacoby, R. (1975) *Social Amnesia: A Critique of Conformist Psychology from Adler to Laing*. New York: Beacon.

Jacoby, R. (1983) *The Repression of Psychoanalysis*. New York: Basic Books.

Jay, M. (1986) 'In the empire of the gaze: Foucault and the denigration of vision in 20th century French thought', in L. Appignanesi (ed.) *Postmodernism, ICA Documents 4*. London: Institute for Contemporary Arts.

Johnstone, A. (2001) 'The vicious circle of the super-ego: The pathological trap of guilt and the beginning of ethics', *Psychoanalytic Studies*, 3(3/4), 411–424.

Kojève, A. (1969) *Introduction to the Reading of Hegel: Lectures on the Phenomenology of Spirit*. New York: Basic Books.

Koyré, A. (1965) *Newtonian Studies*. London: Chapman and Hall.

Kuhn, T. (1962) *The Structure of Scientific Revolutions*. Chicago: University of Chicago Press.

Kvale, S. (ed.) (1992) *Psychology and Postmodernism*. London: Sage.

Kvale, S. (2003) 'The psychoanalytic interview as inspiration for qualitative research', in P. Camic, J. Rhodes and L. Yardley (eds) *Qualitative Research in Psychology: Expanding Perspectives in Methodology and Design*. Washington DC: American Psychological Association Press.

Kvale, S. and Greness, C.E. (1975) 'Skinner and Sartre: Towards a radical phenomenology of behavior', in A. Giorgi, C.T. Fischer and E.L. Murray (eds) *Duquesne Studies in Phenomenological Psychology (Vol. II)*. Pittsburgh: Duquesne University Press.

Lacan, J. (1938) 'Family complexes in the formation of the individual', unpublished translation by Cormac Gallagher from 'La Famille' in *Encyclopédie Francaise*, 8. (Versions of the Gallagher translation are updated from time to time and available at http://www.lacaninireland.com.)

Lacan, J. (1949) 'The mirror stage as formative of the *i* function as revealed in psychoanalytic experience', in J. Lacan (2006) *Écrits: The First Complete Edition in English* (translated with notes by B. Fink in collaboration with H. Fink and R. Grigg). New York: Norton.

Lacan, J. (1952) 'Intervention on transference', in J. Mitchell and J. Rose (eds) (1982) *Feminine Sexuality: Jacques Lacan and the école freudienne*. London: Macmillan.

Lacan, J. (1953) 'The function and field of speech and language in psychoanalysis', in J. Lacan (2006) *Écrits: The First Complete Edition in English* (translated with notes by B. Fink in collaboration with H. Fink and R. Grigg). New York: Norton.

Lacan, J. (1956) 'The Freudian Thing, or the meaning of the return to Freud in psychoanalysis', in J. Lacan (2006) *Écrits: The First Complete Edition in English* (translated with notes by B. Fink in collaboration with H. Fink and R. Grigg). New York: Norton.

Lacan, J. (1956/1972) 'Seminar on "The purloined letter"', *Yale French Studies*, 48, 38–72.

Lacan, J. (1957) 'The instance of the letter in the unconscious, or reason since Freud', in J. Lacan (2006) *Écrits: The First Complete Edition in English* (translated with notes by B. Fink in collaboration with H. Fink and R. Grigg). New York: Norton.

Lacan, J. (1961–1962) *The Seminar of Jacques Lacan Book IX, Identification* (translated from unedited French manuscripts by C. Gallagher), unpublished. (Versions of the Gallagher translation are updated from time to time and available at http://www.lacaninireland.com.)

Lacan, J. (1964/1973) *The Four Fundamental Concepts of Psycho-Analysis: The Seminar of Jacques Lacan, Book XI* (translated by A. Sheridan). Harmondsworth: Penguin.

Lacan, J. (1966) 'Position of the unconscious: remarks made at the 1960 Bonneval colloquium rewritten in 1964' (translated by B. Fink), in R. Feldstein, B. Fink and M. Jaanus (eds) (1995) *Reading Seminar XI: Lacan's Four Fundamental Concepts of Psychoanalysis*. New York: SUNY Press.

Lacan, J. (1973) 'Of structure as an inmixing of an otherness prerequisite to any subject whatever', in R. Macksay and E. Donato (eds) *The Structuralist*

114   *References*

Controversy: The Languages of Criticism and the Sciences of Man. Baltimore, MD: Johns Hopkins Press.

Lacan, J. (1975/1991) *The Seminar of Jacques Lacan: Book I, Freud's Papers on Technique, 1953–1954* (translated by J. Forrester). New York: Norton.

Lacan, J. (1975/1998) *On Feminine Sexuality, The Limits of Love and Knowledge, 1972–1973: Encore, The Seminar of Jacques Lacan, Book XX* (translated by B. Fink). New York: Norton.

Lacan, J. (1977) *Ecrits: A Selection* (translated by A. Sheridan). London: Tavistock Press.

Lacan, J. (1981/1993) *The Psychoses: The Seminar of Jacques Lacan, Book III: 1955–1956* (translated with notes by R. Grigg). London and New York: Routledge.

Lacan, J. (1986/1992) *The Ethics of Psychoanalysis 1959–1960: The Seminar of Jacques Lacan, Book VII* (translated by D. Porter). London: Routledge.

Lacan, J. (1991/2007) *The Other Side of Psychoanalysis: The Seminar of Jacques Lacan, Book XVII* (translated by R. Grigg). New York: Norton.

Lacan, J. (2006) *Écrits: The First Complete Edition in English* (translated with notes by B. Fink, in collaboration with H. Fink and R. Grigg) New York: Norton.

Lacan, J. (2007) *The Other Side of Psychoanalysis: The Seminar of Jacques Lacan, Book XVII* (translated with notes by R. Grigg, originally published 1991). New York: Norton.

Laclau, E. and Mouffe, C. (1985) *Hegemony and Socialist Strategy.* London: Verso.

Laplanche, J. and Leclaire, S. (1972) 'The unconscious: A psychoanalytic study', *Yale French Studies*, 48, 118–175.

Laplanche, J. and Pontalis, J.-B. (1972) 'Appendices (excerpts from *Vocabulaire de la psychanalyse*', *Yale French Studies*, 48, 179–202.

Laplanche, J. and Pontalis, J.-B. (1988) *The Language of Psychoanalysis.* London: Karnac Books and the Institute of Psycho-Analysis.

Lasch, C. (1978) *The Culture of Narcissism: American Life in an Age of Diminishing Expectations.* New York: Norton.

Latour, B. (2000) 'When things strike back: a possible contribution of science studies', *British Journal of Sociology*, 51(1), 107–123.

Lave, J. (1988) *Cognition in Practice.* Cambridge: Cambridge University Press.

Leader, D. (2000) *Freud's Footnotes.* London: Faber and Faber.

Leader, D. and Groves, J. (1995) *Lacan for Beginners.* London: Icon Books.

Lévi-Strauss, C. (1962/1966) *The Savage Mind.* London: Weidenfeld and Nicolson.

Lindsay, P. and Norman, D. (1972) *Human Information Processing: An Introduction to Psychology.* New York: Academic Press.

Lyotard, J.-F. (1979/1984) *The Postmodern Condition: A Report on Knowledge.* Manchester: Manchester University Press.

Macey, D. (1988) *Lacan in Contexts.* London: Verso.

MacCorquodale, K. (1969) 'B.F. Skinner's *Verbal Behavior*: A retrospective appreciation', *Journal of the Experimental Analysis of Behavior*, 12, 831–841.

Malone, K. and Friedlander, S. (eds) (2000) *The Subject of Lacan: A Lacanian Reader for Psychologists.* New York: SUNY Press.

Mandel, E. (1974) *Late Capitalism.* London: New Left Books.

Manning, P. (2005) *Freud and American Sociology*. Cambridge: Polity Press.

Mannoni, O. (1991) *Prospero and Caliban: The Psychology of Colonization*. Ann Arbor: University of Michigan Press.

Marsden, J. (1999) 'Cyberpsychosis: The feminization of the post-biological body', in A.J. Gordo-López and I. Parker (eds) *Cyberpsychology*. London: Palgrave.

Middleton, D. and Edwards, D. (eds) (1990) *Collective Remembering*. London: Sage.

Miller, J.-A. (1986) '*Extimité*', in M. Bracher, M.W. Alcorn, R.J. Corthell and F. Massardier-Kenney (eds) (1994) *Lacanian Theory of Discourse: Subject, Structure and Society*, New York: New York University Press.

Miller, J.-A. and Etchegoyen, H. (1996) 'Silence broken', *Revista Argentina de Psiquiatría*, 7(26), 260–274, http://www.ilimit.com/amp/english/vertex.htm (accessed 3 November 1999).

Miller, L., Rustin, M., Rustin, M. and Shuttleworth, J. (eds) (1989) *Closely Observed Infants*. London: Duckworth.

Mitchell, P. (1992) *The Psychology of the Child*. London: Falmer.

Moscovici, S. (1976/2008) *Psychoanalysis: Its Image and Its Public*. Cambridge: Polity Press.

Muller, J. (1996) *Beyond the Psychoanalytic Dyad: Developmental Semiotics in Freud, Peirce and Lacan*. New York: Routledge.

Nasio, J.-D. (1998) *Five Lessons on the Psychoanalytic Theory of Jacques Lacan*. New York: SUNY Press.

Neill, C. (2015) *Ethics and Psychology: Beyond Codes of Practice*. Abingdon: Routledge.

Nobus, D. (ed.) (1998) *Key Concepts of Lacanian Psychoanalysis*. London: Rebus Press.

Nobus, D. (2000) *Jacques Lacan and the Freudian Practice of Psychoanalysis*. London: Routledge.

Nobus, D. and Quinn, M. (2005) *Knowing Nothing, Staying Stupid: Elements for a Psychoanalytic Epistemology*. London and New York: Routledge.

Packer, M.J. (1985) 'Hermeneutic inquiry in the study of human conduct', *American Psychologist*, 40(10), 1081–1093.

Parker, I. (1989) *The Crisis in Modern Social Psychology, and How to End It*. London/New York: Routledge.

Parker, I. (1992) *Discourse Dynamics: Critical Analysis for Social and Individual Psychology*. London/New York: Routledge.

Parker, I. (1997a) 'Discourse analysis and psycho-analysis', *British Journal of Social Psychology*, 36, 479–495.

Parker, I. (1997b) *Psychoanalytic Culture: Psychoanalytic Discourse in Western Society*. London: Sage.

Parker, I. (1998) 'Against postmodernism: Psychology in cultural context', *Theory & Psychology*, 8(5), 621–647.

Parker, I. (1999a) 'Critical psychology: Critical links', *Annual Review of Critical Psychology*, 1, 3–18.

Parker, I. (1999b) 'Critical reflexive humanism and critical constructionist psychology', in D.J. Nightingale and J. Cromby (eds) *Social Constructionist Psychology:*

116   *References*

A Critical Analysis of Theory and Practice. Buckingham: Open University
Press.

Parker, I. (2000) 'Looking for Lacan: virtual psychology', in K. Malone and S.
Friedlander (eds) *The Subject of Lacan: A Lacanian Reader for Psychologists.*
New York: SUNY Press.

Parker, I. (2001) 'Essay Review of Billig, M. (1999) *Freudian Repression: Conversation Creating the Unconscious', Journal of Community and Applied Social Psychology*, 11(1), 69–73.

Parker, I. (2002) *Critical Discursive Psychology.* London: Palgrave.

Parker, I. (2003) 'Therapy versus Lacanian psychoanalysis', *International Journal of Critical Psychology*, 7, 170–172.

Parker, I. (2004) *Slavoj Žižek: A Critical Introduction.* London: Pluto Press.

Parker, I. (2005) *Qualitative Psychology: Introducing Radical Research.* Buckingham: Open University Press.

Parker, I. (2007) *Revolution in Psychology: Alienation to Emancipation.* London: Pluto Press.

Parker, I. (ed.) (2011a) *Critical Psychology: Critical Concepts in Psychology* (4 vols). Abingdon/New York: Routledge.

Parker, I. (2011b) *Lacanian Psychoanalysis: Revolutions in Subjectivity.* London and New York: Routledge.

Parker, I. and the Bolton Discourse Network (1999) *Critical Textwork: An Introduction to Varieties of Discourse and Analysis.* Buckingham: Open University Press.

Plon, M. (1974) 'On the meaning of the notion of conflict and its study in social psychology', in I. Parker (ed.) (2011) *Critical Psychology: Critical Concepts in Psychology, Vol. 2, Contradictions in Psychology and Elements of Resistance.* Abingdon/New York: Routledge.

Poe, E.A. (1844/1938) 'The purloined letter', in *The Complete Tales and Poems of Edgar Allen Poe.* New York: Random House.

Politzer, G. (1994) *Critique of the Foundations of Psychology: The Psychology of Psychoanalysis.* Pittsburgh, PA.: Duquesne University Press.

Potter, J. (1996) *Representing Reality.* London: Sage.

Potter, J. and Wetherell, M. (1987) *Discourse and Social Psychology: Beyond Attitudes and Behaviour.* London: Sage.

Quackelbeen, J. (1997) 'The psychoanalytic discourse theory of Jacques Lacan: Introduction and application', *Studies in Psychoanalytic Theory*, 3(1), 21–43.

Racevskis, K. (1983) *Michel Foucault and the Subversion of Intellect.* Ithaca, NY: Cornell University Press.

Rajchman, J. (1991) *Truth and Eros: Foucault, Lacan, and the Question of Ethics.* New York: Routledge.

Rayban, C. (1995) *Virtual Sexual Reality.* London: Bodley Head.

Reason, P. and Rowan, J. (eds) (1981) *Human Inquiry: A Sourcebook of New Paradigm Research.* Chichester: Wiley.

Richardson, W.J. (1980) 'Piaget, Lacan and language', in H.J. Silverman (ed. *Piaget, Philosophy and the Human Sciences.* Brighton: Harvester.

Rogers, C.R. (1961) *On Becoming a Person.* Boston: Houghton Mifflin.

Rorty, R. (1980) *Philosophy and the Mirror of Nature.* Oxford: Basil Blackwell.

Rose, N. (1985) *The Psychological Complex: Psychology, Politics and Society in England 1869–1939.* London: Routledge and Kegan Paul.

Roudinesco, E. (1990) *Jacques Lacan and Co.: A History of Psychoanalysis in France, 1925–1985.* London: Free Association Books.

Rushkoff, D. (1994) *Cyberia: Life in the Trenches of Hyperspace.* London: Flamingo.

Saito, T. (2003) *The Psychologization of Society: Why Trauma and Healing are Desired.* Tokyo: PHP.

Sarup, M. (1988) *An Introductory Guide to Post-structuralism and P ostmodernism.* Hassocks, Sussex: Harvester Wheatsheaf.

Saussure, F. de (1915/1974) *Course in General Linguistics.* Glasgow: Fontana/Collins.

Shannon, C. and Weaver, W. (1949) *The Mathematical Theory of Communication.* Urbana: University of Illinois Press.

Shields, R. (ed.) (1996) *Cultures of Internet: Virtual Spaces, Real Histories, Living Bodies.* London: Sage.

Shingu, K. (2004) *Being Irrational: Lacan, the Objet a, and the Golden Mean* (translated and edited by M. Radich). Tokyo: Gakuju Shoin.

Shotter, J. (1975) *Images of Man in Psychological Research.* London: Methuen.

Silverman, H.J. (ed.) (1980) *Piaget, Philosophy and the Human Sciences.* Brighton: Harvester.

Skinner, B.F. (1950) 'Are theories of learning necessary?' *Psychological Review,* 57, 193–216.

Skinner, B.F. (1953) *Science and Human Behavior.* New York: Free Press.

Skinner, B.F. (1957) *Verbal Behavior.* London: Methuen.

Skinner, B.F. (1973) *Beyond Freedom and Dignity.* Harmondsworth: Penguin.

Skinner, B.F. (1977) 'Why I am not a cognitive psychologist', *Behaviourism,* 5(2), 1–10.

Soler, C. (1995) 'The body in the teaching of Jacques Lacan', *Journal of the Centre for Freudian Analysis and Research,* 6, 6–38.

Stavrakakis, Y. (1999) *Lacan and the Political.* London: Routledge.

Stern, D.N. (1985) *The Interpersonal World of the Infant: A View from Psychoanalysis and Developmental Psychology.* New York: Basic Books.

Thom, M. (1976) 'The unconscious structured like a language', *Economy & Society,* 5, 435–469.

Trower, P., Bryant, P. and Argyle, M. (1978) *Social Skills and Mental Health.* London: Methuen.

Verhaeghe, P. (1995) 'From impossibility to inability: Lacan's theory on the four discourses', *The Letter,* 3, 76–99.

Verhaeghe, P. (1999) *Does the Woman Exist? From Freud's Hysteric to Lacan's Feminine.* London: Rebus Press.

Vološinov, V.N. (1927/1973) *Marxism and the Philosophy of Language.* New York: Seminar Press.

Vorsteg, R.H. (1974) 'Operant reinforcement theory and determinism', *Behaviourism,* 3(1), 108–119.

Walkerdine, V. (1982) 'From context to text: A psychosemiotic approach to abstract thought', in M. Beveridge (ed.) *Children Thinking Through Language*. London: Edward Arnold.

Wallace, P. (1999) *The Psychology of the Internet*. Cambridge: Cambridge University Press.

Wann, T.W. (1964) (ed.) *Behaviorism and Phenomenology: Contrasting Bases for Modern Psychology*. Chicago: University of Chicago Press.

Watson, J.B. (1913) 'Psychology as the behaviorist views it', *Psychological Review*, 20, 158–177.

Wetherell, M. and Potter, J. (1992) *Mapping the Language of Racism*. Hemel Hempstead: Harvester Wheatsheaf.

Winograd, T. and Flores, F. (1987) *Understanding Computers and Cognition: A New Foundation for Design*. Reading, MA: Addison-Wesley.

Žižek, S. (1999) *The Ticklish Subject: The Absent Centre of Political Ontology*. London: Verso.

Index

absolutization 89, 91, 92
action research 67
activity theory 16, 25
acts, ethical 85, 88
affect 76
agency 47–48, 99
agents 31, 35, 39, 41, 43, 59, 107
aggressivity 51
Althusser, Louis 49
American Psychoanalytic
    Association 93–94
anaclitic nature of speech 60
animal communication 47
animal ethology 27
anthropological space 94–96, 99, 106
anthropology 66–67, 75, 77, 96, 103
anti-humanism 44
anti-psychoanalysis 62, 63, 73, 75, 80
anti-psychology 62, 80, 86, 92, 99
Aristotle 83, 86
art 88, 90–91, 92, 103
artificial intelligence (AI) 18
autoclitic behaviour 53, 57, 59, 60

Badiou, Alain 82–83, 86–91, 92
'barred psychologist' 13, 14, 27–28, 29
'barred subject' 18, 22, 24, 28, 31,
    39–40, 41
behaviourism 15, 19, 44, 45, 46–61,
    84; *see also* Skinner
'Being' 17, 18, 52–53
Bentham, Jeremy 84, 87
Betrayal 89, 90, 91, 92
Bettelheim, Bruno 49
Blackman, D.E. 46
Body 18, 71, 107

Bolsheviks 88–89
boundaries 78
British Psychological Society 37–38,
    41

capitalism 68, 76, 88, 97, 98, 105,
    106
Cartesian dualism 15, 17
castration 8
Catania, A.C. 50
categorical imperative 84, 86
Chandra, S. 53–54
child development 20–22
child psychoanalysis 27
Choang-tsu 101
clinical practice 9, 10, 13, 27, 34, 65,
    69
cogito 17–18
cognition 15–19, 20, 24, 51–53
cognitive psychology 15–19, 52, 54
collective memory 24–25
collective unconscious 104
commonsense 97–98
communication 4, 16, 24
community 87, 89
conditioning 46–47
'conditions of possibility' 31
confession 64
conflict 65, 78
consciousness 53–55, 99, 100, 102
constructionism 1, 24–25, 31, 56, 103
consumer culture 68, 98
conversation analysis 25
conversion hysteria 18, 71
counselling 10
counter-transference 9, 77

Marxism 42, 63–64, 65, 71, 77, 80–81
master signifiers 30–31, 35–37, 39, 41, 43
master/slave dialectic 51
materialism 103–104
mathemes 22, 28
meaning 16–17, 25, 48, 58, 64, 71; conventionality of 80; interpretation 74–75, 76, 79; 'turn to' 67–70
mediation 63
memory 15, 17, 54; collective 24–25; of trauma 21
mentalism 60
metaphor 47, 54, 57, 58
method 72, 78, 79–80
metonymy 47, 57, 58
Miller, Jacques-Alain 2
mirror stage 20, 27, 52
miscommunication 13
Möbius strip 22–23
modernity 97
mother-infant relationship 21
Mouffe, Chantal 85

narcissism 98
Nazism 88–89
neurosis 5, 6, 7, 101
'new paradigm' 23, 40

objectivity 77
object-relations theory 25–26
objects 25–26, 40, 86; cyberspace 100–101; Foucauldian discourse analysis 31, 32; lost 4, 8; Marxist approaches 64; psychological knowledge 38–39; science-art divide 91
objet petit a 25–26, 28, 31, 38–39, 40, 41
obsessional neurosis 6
October Revolution 88–89, 90
Oedipal myth 8
operant behaviour 46–47, 49, 50
the Other 21–22; cross-cultural psychology 95; desire of 8, 51; discourse of 4, 16, 17, 104; ethics 86–87; gaze of 101, 102; psychological knowledge 35, 38

'paradigm crisis' 66
'paradigm revolutions' 42
parapraxes 48
participant research 67
perverse structure 5, 6–7
phallus 8, 47
phenomenology 23, 45, 51, 52, 54, 55
Piaget, Jean 20
Poe, Edgar Allen 24
politics 3–4, 65, 88–90, 98
Politzer, Georges 62, 80
Pontalis, J.-B. 60
popular culture 68–69, 71, 72, 79, 103
positivism 24, 36, 68, 86
'postmodern condition' 95
postmodernism 24, 98–99, 100
post-structuralism 24, 44, 58, 61, 64, 65–66, 77, 81
power 8–9, 64
private stimuli 55–57, 59
psychiatry 10, 42, 68
psychoanalysis 13, 30, 62–63, 65–71; aim of 52–53; anti-psychoanalysis 62, 63, 73, 75, 80; anti-psychology 86; application of 70–71; comparison with behaviourism 49; cyberspace 93–94, 99–107; determinism 48; disavowal of indebtedness to 66–67; ethics 83, 84; inside/outside dichotomy 22; interiority 75–76; interpretation 73–75; Lacan on 14, 21, 27, 29; language and 44–45; psy-complex 42; relationships 78–79; repression of 55; researcher subjectivity 77; the self 61; socio-critical strategies 79–81; subversiveness 3; turn to meaning 67–70; *see also* Lacanian psychoanalysis
psychologization 2, 69, 75–76, 78, 79
psychology 12–13, 14, 27–28, 29, 66; anti-psychology 62, 80, 92, 99; cognitive 15–19, 52, 54; computer technology 94; crisis in 60; cross-cultural 34, 95; cyberspace 96–98; developmental 20–22, 26, 68, 73; discourse analysis 31–32; discourse of the university 30, 33–37, 42–43; ethics 82–85, 90–92;